OCCASIONAL PUBLICATIONS OF THE

DEPARTMENT OF NEAR EASTERN STUDIES

AND THE

PROGRAM OF JEWISH STUDIES

CORNELL UNIVERSITY

Edited by

Ross Brann
and
David I. Owen

Editorial Committee

Ross Brann,
David I. Owen,
David S. Powers,
Gary A. Rendsburg

Isaac Rabinowitz
1909-1988

# A WITNESS FOREVER

*Ancient Israel's*
*Perception of Literature*
*and the Resultant Hebrew Bible*

## Isaac Rabinowitz

EDITED WITH AFTERWORDS BY
Ross Brann and David I. Owen

WITHDRAWN
C D L Press   Bethesda, MD

Library of Congress Cataloging-in-Publication Data

Rabinowitz, Isaac, 1909-1988
   A witness forever : ancient Israel's perception of literature
and the resultant Hebrew Bible / Isaac Rabinowitz ;
edited with afterwords by Ross Brann and David I. Owen.
      p.   cm. — (Occasional publications of the Department
of Near Eastern Studies and the Program of Jewish Studies,
Cornell University ; v. 1)
   Includes bibliographical references and index.
   ISBN 1-88305-302-1 : $20.00
   1. Bible.   O.T. —Criticism, interpretation, etc.   2. Bible.
O.T.—Sources.   3. Bible as literature.   I. Brann, Ross, 1949-
II. Owen, David I.   III. Title.   IV. Series.
BS1171.2.R29   1993
221.6'6—dc20                                    93-36513
                                                   CIP

SBN 1-88305-302-1

# PREFACE

This volume begins an occasional publications series of the Department of Near Eastern Studies and the Program of Jewish Studies at Cornell University.

In 1932, as a direct consequence of the Great Depression and coincident with the retirement of Professor Nathaniel Schmidt, the Department of Semitic Languages and Literatures and Oriental History was disbanded. It was not until 1965 that the Department of Semitic Languages and Literatures was reinstated under the chairmanship of Professor Isaac Rabinowitz. In 1972, when Professor Benzion Netanyahu joined the department, the Program of Jewish Studies was established as an extension of the department. In 1976, shortly after Professor David I. Owen joined the faculty and became chair, the name of the department was changed to Near Eastern Studies to reflect the expansion of the curriculum which now included Biblical studies, Near Eastern and Biblical history and archaeology, Assyriology, Islamic literature and history, Hebrew and Arabic. The Program of Jewish Studies became a university program and incorporated courses traditionally beyond the scope of Near Eastern Studies. Since that time, the Department and the Program's faculty have grown slowly as have their respective curriculums. This series will reflect the diverse research activities of the faculty associated with both the Department and the Program along with other relevant topics. It is fitting that the first volume be a manuscript left by Isaac Rabinowitz at his death in 1988. Without his commitment, neither the Department nor the Program would have likely come into being again. It is our hope that subsequent volumes will continue to emulate the high standards and meticulous scholarship which is the legacy of Isaac Rabinowitz.

Publication of this volume was made possible by a generous subvention from the Lucius N. Littauer Foundation. We wish to express our sincere thanks to William L. Frost, president, and Pamela Ween Brumberg, program officer, for their interest and support of this endeavor. Dr. Mark Cohen of CDL Press facilitated the rapid production of this handsome volume from computer files expertly compiled by Ms. Lesli LaRocco from the original manuscript. We thank them both for their dedication and effort. Finally, we wish to note the devotion of Mr. Joel Rabinowitz, who provided us with his father's manuscript, helped to compile the preliminary bibliography, carefully checked the references, and read the proofs. His efforts are a fitting tribute to his father's memory.

Ross Brann
David I. Owen
Ithaca, New York
May 28, 1993

לרביתן,

Alice Elson Rabinowitz, ז"ל

מְשׂוֹשׂ חַיָּי

*Come and write it now on a tablet of theirs,*
*and inscribe it upon a book,*
*that it may constitute, at a later date,*
*a witness forever.*

(Isaiah 30:8)

# TABLE OF CONTENTS

### ANCIENT ISRAEL'S BELIEF ABOUT WORDS:
### HOW THE CREATORS OF THE HEBREW BIBLE PERCEIVED
### THE MEDIUM OF LITERATURE

1. Preliminary Considerations   2. The Presumed Nature of Words   3. The Presumed Properties and Powers of Words 4. "Holy Words"

### ANCIENT ISRAEL'S BELIEFS
### ABOUT THE LITERARY PROCESS

1. Literacy  2. "Reading"  3. "Writing"  4. "Book"  5. Literary Witness  6. Some Possible Misconceptions of the Argument of this Book

### SOME "ANOMALOUS" LITERARY AND RHETORICAL
### CONSEQUENCES OF ANCIENT ISRAEL'S
### PERCEPTION OF LITERATURE

1. Words as Future Historical "Realities" 2. Words Directed to Unwitting or Insentient Addressees   3. Wishes or Hopes Stated as Accomplished Actualities   4. The "Booking" of Future "Realities"   5. The Reading-out of "Booked Realities" as Means of their Effectuation

# FOREWORD

*One must beware of hindsight and stereotypes. More gene-*
*rally one must beware of the error that consists in judging dis-*
*tant epochs and places with the yardstick that prevails in the*
*here and now, an error all the more difficult to avoid as the dis-*
*tance in space and time increases. This is the reason why, for*
*us who are not specialists, comprehending biblical and Hom-*
*eric texts or even the Greek and Latin Classics is so arduous*
*an undertaking.*

Primo Levi,
*The Drowned and the Saved*
(New York, 1988), 165

How was literature perceived in the culture that
produced the Hebrew Scriptures, or Old Testament? To
answer this basic question—to clarify and make explicit for
modern readers what persons native to ancient Israel's
culture assumed, believed, took for granted about literature
as they wrote and read literary texts, including the texts now
before us in the Hebrew Bible—is the primary purpose of this
essay.[1]

Such clarification, I believe, is basic and indispensable to
all study of the Scriptures that seeks to understand them as
their ancient creators and transmitters meant them to be

---

[1] Unless otherwise noted, all Scriptural quotations in this book have
been translated by the writer from the Massoretic text of the Hebrew
Bible. Readers will find it profitable and interesting to compare these
renderings with those of the various standard translations. The occasion-
ally different numbering of verses in the King James Version, the Revised
Standard Version, and the New English Bible is given in parentheses, e.g.,
Hosea 2:1(1:10).

understood. The beliefs about literature that are held and handed down in a given culture—beliefs about what literature is, what it can accomplish, and how it works—naturally condition, define, even engender the literature of that culture. These beliefs and assumptions, like other traditional patterns of thought and action, are not necessarily everywhere and always the same, but may differ from culture to culture. Thus, the assumptions that governed the production and reception of literature in ancient Israel's culture were not, as we shall see, the same as those of our English-speaking and other western cultures. If, accordingly, we wish to try to understand the texts of the Hebrew Bible as their ancient Israelite producers originally intended them to be understood, we must learn to read them in the light of how the literary art was perceived in ancient Israel. To neglect these underlying taken-for-granted presumptions—rather, as usually is done in modern treatments of the Bible as literature, to read the Hebrew Scriptures in the light of our quite different western cultural assumptions and expectations as to the nature and functioning of literature—must inevitably result in misunderstanding and misinterpretation of the originally intended sense and significance of the Scriptural texts. It is as a contribution to the avoidance of cultural fallaciousness and exegetical anachronism in modern study of the literature of the Hebrew Bible that this essay is intended.

In seeking to describe and exemplify the beliefs and assumptions involved in ancient Israel's perception of literature, recourse must be had to the Scriptural texts themselves. We have, after all, no better means of access to the culturally significant premises of ancient Israel's practice and reception of the literary art. The scribes who wrote and edited the texts have unfortunately left us no overt statements of what they believed about the nature, purposes and functioning of literature. We must, therefore, assemble this vitally important information from the clues left in the textual results of their scribal productivity, as these are now still available to us.

Chapters One and Two of the present essay set forth the key assumptions—different, it will be realized, from those of our western literate cultures—that were taken for granted in ancient Israel about the nature and powers of words (the medium of literature), and about the composition and functioning of bodies of written words, or texts. The next two chapters, Three and Four, are devoted to demonstrating the usefulness of the ancient postulation in clarifying and explaining an entire range of rhetorical and textual "anomalies" and difficulties within the Scriptures. Each instance of such clarification or resolution is, of course, further evidence that the ancient set of beliefs is fully operative in the Hebrew Bible. In Chapters Five and Six, finally, aspects of the ancient perception are shown to bear upon, and to help solve, two "higher critical" Biblical problems: (1) the nature, contents and functioning of a named source (*The Book of the Upright*) that was drawn upon by the writer and editors who composed a major portion of the Hebrew Bible; and (2) the originally intended literary unity of the assembled Hebrew Scriptures.

Both smaller-scale and larger-scale problems of Old Testament interpretation are thus found amenable to solution when studied in terms of the beliefs and assumptions about literature handed down in the culture of ancient Israel. Those beliefs and assumptions will, indeed, be found pertinent, if not indispensable, to the consideration not only of passages which obviously contain phenomena that are seemingly hard or impossible to explain, but also of many of the passages which seem to us quite "normal," and not at all strange or exceptional in terms of our modern expectations as to literature. No more has been done in this essay, however, than I have thought needful to prove the utility of the approach *via* ancient Israel's perception of the literature to the study and understanding of the Hebrew Bible.

This approach to the Hebrew Scriptures, it must be pointed out, differs radically from any other that has thus far appeared in Biblical scholarship. For strange as it may seem, while some of the beliefs that comprise ancient Israel's postulation of literature—particularly, the assumptions respecting the extra-communicative powers of words—have long been known, their importance and utility for the understanding and interpretation of Biblical Hebrew literature as such have hitherto gone all but unrecognized and unstudied. There have been almost no attempts by Biblical scholars to bring ancient Israel's own perception of literature to bear upon the literary and textual problems of the Hebrew Scriptures.[2]

But if the approach is new and almost unheard of in modern Biblical scholarship, I nevertheless believe that its insights need not and should not be confined to the comparatively restricted readership of professional Biblical scholars. I have accordingly addressed this work to all readers who may be interested in trying to find out how those who wrote and edited the Hebrew Scriptures meant them to be understood. The book is neither overburdened with references to professional scholarship, whether "pro" or "con" its own arguments and findings, nor does it presuppose acquaintance with the "original tongues" (Hebrew and Aramaic) of the Old Testament, nor any other specialized knowledge or skills. I have tried to write it so that any person who can read straightforward English, and is willing to think about what he or she is reading, can understand it. Indeed, the approach to the understanding of Biblical literature set forth in these pages is mainly the product of my attempts, through many years, to help undergraduate students in a course on the Hebrew Bible at Cornell University ("all texts will be read in English translation") achieve such understanding. My experience in teaching Cornell undergraduates encourages me to think that other interested readers of the Bible will also find this means of access to the ancient texts helpful. A not inconsiderable advantage of the approach, I have found, is that its objective

---

[2] So far as I am aware, my own two preliminary papers—"Towards a Valid Theory of Biblical Hebrew Literature" (in L. Wallach, ed., *The Classical Tradition: Literary and Historical Studies in Honor of Harry Caplan* [Ithaca, N.Y., 1966], 315-328), and "'Word' and Literature in Ancient Israel" (*New Literary History*, IV [1972-1973], 119-139)—are thus far the only published studies that approach Biblical Hebrew literary and textual problems from the vantage-point of ancient Israel's culturally distinctive postulation of literature. This neglect on the part of Biblical scholars is the more surprising in that the anthropologist's "culture-oriented" approach has been used to great advantage in the study of many other aspects of ancient Israel's life and thought.

validity makes it one which votaries of every religious point of view, or of none, can join in using.

It is a pleasure here to acknowledge my gratitude to the National Endowment for the Humanities for the senior fellowship which, in 1971-1972, enabled me to explore and to define various aspects of ancient Israel's postulation of literature. I am also indebted to my late wife, Alice, and to my son, Joel B. Rabinowitz, for their helpful suggestions on the argument and style of the book; and to the Humanities Faculty Research Grants Committee of the College of Arts and Sciences, Cornell University, for a grant of the funds needed for preparation of the manuscript for publication.

Isaac Rabinowitz

# CHAPTER ONE

## ANCIENT ISRAEL'S BELIEFS ABOUT WORDS:

### HOW THE CREATORS OF THE HEBREW BIBLE
### PERCEIVED THE MEDIUM OF LITERATURE

The two sets of socially learned and transmitted assumptions most crucially and intimately involved in the matter and manner of literary productivity in ancient Israel, as in any literate human culture, are, first, those concerning the nature and powers of words in general, and second, those involved in the process of composing, writing down, and reading of bodies of ordered words, that is to say, of *texts*. As the examples from the Hebrew Bible that I shall present in these chapters clearly demonstrate, the ancient Israelite beliefs in regard to these matters are not inevitably and invariably the same as those generally held in our modern western societies. This disparity, indeed, is what basically accounts for much of the strangeness, the bizarreness, one might almost say the incomprehensibility, of Old Testament texts when considered and studied as we in the West today habitually approach and study "literature." If, however, we read those texts in the light of the cultural assumptions described in this chapter and the next, we shall, I think, find that their strangeness as "literature" is considerably mitigated.

### 1. *Preliminary Considerations*

Since literature consists of words wrought into structures—since words are the medium of literature—a given society's or culture's perception of literature will primarily depend on the beliefs about the nature and powers of words prevalent in that society or culture. Those beliefs may, of course, be consciously formulated and held, as among modern linguists, psychologists and philosophers. Basically, however, and far more commonly, the beliefs involved are just taken for granted: their origins lie too far back in the history of most cultures to be identified. However and by whomever initiated, they are assumptions, traditionally handed down in a particular society or culture along with transmission of its language. Notions and intimations as to what words are, as to their properties and powers, are caught and absorbed by successive generations of speakers of a language as they learn the various culturally determined modes and relationships in which words can, must, or should be used. In the case of an extinct literate culture like that of ancient Israel, if we wish to find out what native speakers of its language—classical Hebrew, the main language of the Old Testament—took for granted about the nature and power of words, we must examine the references to words in its surviving literary texts, note how words are described or exhibited as functioning, and, particularly and especially, try to grasp the nature of the relationship assumed by the ancient Israelites to obtain between words and the various matters, actions and events—the "realities"—they designate.[3]

Here, since the matter is of such fundamental and vital importance to the content of this book, and indeed to all study and criticism of the Bible, let me anticipate my demonstration and state as succinctly and plainly as I can the essential difference between what we in our modern western societies and cultures take for granted about words in ancient Israel's culture. It is this: we today regard words as almost exclusively the *symbols* in and through which people communicate ideas and feelings with one another; the words *stand for*—represent—the realities, actions and relationships about which information and expression of feeling are thus communicated and exchanged—but the words themselves,

---

[3] A.C. Thiselton, "The Supposed Power of Words in the Biblical Writings" (*Journal of Theological Studies*, XXV [1974], 283-299), quite properly points out (p. 287) that the ancient Israelite "view of words is simply wrong." But the fact that it is wrong—hardly strange, considering that it was not until the 20th century C.E. that the view of words considered by Thiselton to be correct established itself among western linguists, semanticists and philosophers—does not, of course, alter the significant fact that it was the view of words actually held by the ancient Israelites, including the scribes who composed and edited the Hebrew Scriptures.

as *words,* are perceived to be quite other than, quite distinct from, the sensible substantiality of the realities, actions, relationships they stand for. In the culture of ancient Israel, on the other hand, while words indeed did constitute the medium of interpersonal communication and expression, the words were not perceived and thought of as exchangeable *symbols* or *representations* of their sensible referents, but rather as *those referents themselves*—the palpable objects, the "real" and perceptible actions and events, the sensible relationships and interactions—in the *concentrated form* of words.[4] When, in our western cultures, we today find ourselves communicating ideas and feelings, we assume that we are using the voiced air-puffs or inscribed markings of our words as *symbols* of actual or imagined realities. The ancient Israelites assumed, when they spoke and wrote, that they were passing to their hearers or readers the *concentrated essences* of the actual or imagined realities. Like ourselves,

------

[4] Professor James Barr in his *The Scope and Authority of the Bible* (Philadelphia, 1980), 2-3 and 141, is critical of "the often canvassed view that in ancient Israel words had 'power' in a sense foreign to our experience," a view that he considers helped bring about the "decline or decease of the ... biblical theology of the period 1945-1960." "Of course," he writes, "one can find in the Old Testament instances of words, names, and sentences that are conceived as having power, but it is quite unjustified to generalize this into the notion that all words, names, and sentences are so regarded. If they have power, it is because they are the words, names, and sentences of powerful persons, like God, or great kings, prophets and commanders; no one in Israel thought that the word 'egg' or 'mud' conveyed the 'power' of eggs or mud in any way beyond ways found equally among modern men." Presumably, according to Professor Barr, if in the Old Testament God, or a great king, prophet or commander, should be cited as using the word "egg" or "mud," even these words might be "conceived as having power." As pointed out below, the ancient Israelite view of the nature of words and their powers, and of their connectedness with the "realities" which, with us today, they symbolize or represent, is clearly the same, no matter to whom the words are attributed. The degree of "power" in the words may, to be sure, differ from person to person, depending on the power of the "soul" of the utterer; but the view of words as such can certainly not be "symbolic" in the case of some speakers, and "power-laden" in the case of others. Since, as the ancient Israelites viewed the matter, there could be no physical mud without a word "mud," to them physical mud and the word "mud" were just different aspects of the same entity—the latter merely the concentrated essence of the former. A physical or palpable reality we notice is thought of as a "filling" or an "arising from" its word-form; cf. Deut. 9:5 and I Kings 2:27 (cited below).

the ancient Israelites of course believed that words could be
used to convey information, express and communicate feelings and attitudes, persuade, delight. Unlike ourselves,
however, they thought of the words thus used as the
essences, reduced and concentrated for the purposes of such
use, of quite palpable substances, power-instruments,
courses of action. It is to the first belief about the utility of
words that those literary phenomena in the Hebrew Scriptures which seem to us relatively "natural" are traceable, to
the second many of the literary phenomena in those Scriptures that strike us as bizarre and strange.

It should not be supposed—as, in view of the religion-
permeated content of the Hebrew Bible, it is natural for the
modern readers to suppose—that it is only words thought to
have been uttered by God and extraordinarily powerful
human beings that were believed by the ancient Israelites to
possess extra-communicative properties and potencies.[5] As
we shall see, words as such, no matter by whom uttered,
were in that culture regarded as phenomena capable of being
invested with what we today would consider extraordinary
attributes and powers; the fact and the degree of such invest-
ment, however, was thought of as depending upon the
strength of the "soul" in which the words originated, of the
person who uttered them or caused them to be uttered.[6] God,
of course, is infinitely more powerful than any other soul;
His words, therefore, are preeminently charged with these
extraordinary—as they seem to us—properties and powers.
But just as, according to the Scriptures, God, quite like man,
uses words for purposes of communication and expression,
so the words of human beings—especially strong-souled
individuals, like prophets, wise men and women, leading
personalities—might also be invested with extra-communi-

---

[5] This is the view of the matter espoused by Thiselton and Barr in the
works referred to in notes 3 and 4 above. Thiselton writes: "Arguments are
put forward about the nature of *words in general* on the basis of passages which
speak not about words as such but about words which have been uttered
usually *by a god*, or by a king or a prophet" (T.'s italics; p. 290).

[6] J. Pedersen, *Israel: Its Life and Culture* I (London, 1926), 167: "Behind the
word stands the whole of the soul which created it."

cative power. Considering that the writers and editors of the Hebrew Scriptures obviously believed that the "real" nature of any phenomenon is what God has declared or manifested it to be, they could hardly have thought of words, of language—the phenomenon used alike by God and by man—as intrinsically and substantially different for man from what it is for God. The words of a man like Balaam, for instance, could *a priori* be presumed to be powerful enough to procure Israel's defeat at the hands of the Moabites. This was why, we are told in Numbers 22:2ff., Balaam was invited by the Moabite king, Balak, to come and curse Israel. And it is a fact of considerable significance and interest that the narrative in Numbers presents the frustration of Balak's design not through any asserted or demonstrated lack of potency in words when uttered by a mere human being, but rather through the divine intervention whereby the human being, Balaam, is caused to utter the *right kind* of potent words—blessings instead of curses. It is *as words* that the utterances of both God and man, in the belief of the ancient Israelite creators of the Hebrew Scriptures, might be held replete with extra-communicative powers and attributes. The Hebrew Bible, as we shall see, must remain inexplicable as literature if it is not realized that its creators considered words—the literary medium—capable of effects not necessarily restricted to those of communication and expression.

### 2. The Presumed Nature of Words

I proceed now to illustrate, by examples drawn from Biblical Hebrew texts, the difference between ancient Israel's cultural postulation of the nature of words and that of our western societies. The examples I am going to offer are, of course, the merest fraction only of the evidence that might be cited, but they are sufficient, I think, to make clear the nature of words as taken for granted in ancient Israel. They fall into two main groups: (a) those illustrative of the essential inseparability of word and reality in the cultural consciousness of native users of classical Hebrew; and (b) those illustrative of the assumption, culturally received and transmitted by such users, that words are *concentrated essences* or *fundamental inner characters* of their respective real referents.

First, then, some examples of word and reality perceived as inseparable, as indivisible parts of an actuality of some kind. At Numbers 11:23, for instance, we read:

> And the Lord said to Moses, "Is the Lord's hand shortened? Now you shall see whether my word will encounter you or not."

The Lord's "word" here is at one and the same time his previously given promise to give the faithless and murmuring Israelites enough meat for a whole month and the imminent actualizing of that promise. "Encounter" is a literal translation of the term used in the Hebrew text: other possible renderings would be "befall," "meet," "light upon." Note the Hebrew speaks of the *word* "lighting upon," "meeting," "you," i.e., Moses; in English we feel more comfortable in speaking of persons doing the "meeting"—we would rather have the verse read: "Now you shall see whether or not you will experience the fulfillment of my promise." Because, in the Hebrew here, "word" is the subject of "encounter," "you" its object, our several English versions of the Bible try to avoid the awkwardness by employing various circumlocutions. Thus, the King James Version reads "… come to pass unto thee," the Revised Standard Version "… will come true for you or not," the New English Bible "… whether or not my words (*sic*) come true," and the Modern Jewish Version "… whether what I have said happens to you or not." Considering the disparate cultural assumptions as to the nature of words in ancient Israel and in the modern English-speaking world, the circumlocutions employed by the translators in rendering this passage are natural enough. As the context shows, what Moses was to see was the provisioning of the people with meat, the promised realization of the Lord's word. Since we in the English-speaking world habitually conceive of a word as an entity—quite separate and apart from the "real" entity, the actuality, which it symbolizes and designates, we inevitably translate the Hebrew before us here by means of some such circumlocution as "whether … my word will come true for you." In classical Hebrew, however, since in ancient Israel word and reality are not at all sharply discriminated, but are rather perceived and thought of as the same actual entity in different aspects, it is altogether natural and proper to speak of a word's "encountering" or "lighting upon" somebody. Here the total reality bound up in the previously given word—the reality first, indeed, thus adumbrated in its utterance-aspect—is to impinge itself upon, to "encounter" and thus become palpable to, Moses.

The assumed essential inseparability of word and reality is also exhibited at Ezekiel 12:26-28:

> And the word of the Lord came to me, saying: "Son of man, behold, the house of Israel are saying: 'The vision which he sees is many days off, and it is for distant times that he prophesies.' Say to them, therefore, Thus says the Lord God: The whole of My word shall not again be postponed; since I shall speak word that it be enacted, states the Lord God."

What is involved here is, of course, not a postponed utterance, or a postponed completion of some speech, but rather a postponed *actuality*. It is the realities designated by the phrase "the whole of My word" that were previously postponed, but are not to be postponed again. If postponed actuality can be spoken of as postponed "word," it is because word and actuality are by native users of classical Hebrew perceived as essentially the same indivisible entity, so bound up together that the word *is* actuality in this utterable and writable aspect. We note, too, that it is through issuance of another divine word—another "fiat"—that the full actuality of the previously postponed word is to be enacted.

A third instance of the assumption that the word is itself the actuality adumbrated by it figures in the account of Jeremiah's purchase of the field at Anathoth:

> And Jeremiah said: "The word of the Lord came to me, saying: Behold, Hanamel, the son of your uncle Shallum, is going to come to you and say, 'Buy for yourself my field that is at Anathoth, which is in the land of Benjamin, for you have the redemption-right to buy.' And Hanamel, my uncle's son, did come to me, according to the word of the Lord, at the court of the guard, and said to me: 'Now do buy my field that is at Anathoth, which is in the land of Benjamin,

for you have the heirship-right, and the duty to redeem is
yours; buy it for yourself.' So I knew that it was the word
of the Lord: whereupon I purchased from Hanamel, my
uncle's son, the field which is at Anathoth, and weighed him
out the money, seventeen shekels of silver" (Jer. 32:6-9).

Hanamel's *acts*—his coming to Jeremiah and urging the
purchase of the field—are here referred to as "the word of
the Lord" ("So I knew that it was the word of the Lord"), the
actualized word which the prophet recognized as the same
word that had earlier reached him.

Two further instances of the "word"/"actuality" identity
are the following: Jehu, told of the little left of Queen Jezebel
that could be found to bury, says,

"It is the word of the Lord, that which He spoke by His
servant, Elijah ..." (II Kings 9:36).

The Benjaminite who bore the tidings of the battle in which
the Philistines defeated Israel and captured the ark of the
Lord, is asked by Eli, "What was the word, my son?" (I
Samuel 4:16). As the context demonstrates, this means,
"What happened?" "What was the actual outcome?" Eli can
put his question in the form of "What was the word?"
because "actuality" and "word" are considered not two
separate entities, but the same entity: "actuality" is the
completely realized, fulfilled "word," and "word" is "actuality" itself in its utterable aspect.

Because "word," in ancient Israelite consciousness, was
not separable from whatever "real" referent it might designate, the commonest Biblical Hebrew word for "word"—
*dābhār*—may also signify "thing," "affair," "action," "act,"
"fact," "event," "process," "procedure." Translators into the
languages of our modern western societies are, therefore, not
seldom at a loss to know how *dābhār* should be rendered; at
Jer. 20:1, for example, the plural of *dābhār*, as direct object of
the verb "prophesy," is translated "things" by the Revised
Standard Version, but at Jer. 25:30, where the same construction occurs, it is translated "words." More interestingly, we
note that the possible ambiguity to which the "word"/"actuality" identity may give rise could be used rhetorically by

ancient Israelite authors as a *double entendre*. The story of
Ehud's assassination of Eglon, the fat Moabite king (Judges
3:14ff.), in fact turns upon two such *double entendres*. Ehud
first gains private access to the king by saying, "I have a
*dᵉbhar-sēther*"—word/act of secrecy—"unto you, O king";
when he thereafter says, "I have a *dᵉbhar-ʾᵉlōhīm*"—word/
action of God—"unto you," the king out of respect for the
divine, rises from his throne, and so presents himself to
Ehud's sword (Judges 3:19-20). The narrative of David's
slaying of Goliath also contains an instance of the use of such
a *double entendre*. David, inquiring of the Israelite soldiers
what reward would be given whoever might slay the Philis-
tine, and implying that he would accomplish this feat, is
overheard by his older brother, Eliab. Rebuked for presump-
tuousness by Eliab, David replies with two rhetorical questions intended to be understood in both of two ways. "What
have I done now? Is not that word?" he asks, meaning (1)
"I've done nothing but confirm 'word,' that the reward is as
the soldiers are saying," and (2) "I've done nothing as yet,
but is not that—the slaying of Goliath and receiving the
reward—'word,' namely, the actuality-to-be?" (I Samuel
17:24-29).

Our second ancient Israelite assumption regarding the
nature of words—that words were taken to be *concentrated
essences* or *inner character*s of their respective real referents—
is perhaps most strikingly exhibited in a particular usage of
*dābhār* ("word") in Biblical Hebrew. By virtue of this usage,
the fact that the referent of a succeeding expression is distin-
guishably, most characteristically, and intensely itself is
pointed out and emphasized.

Towards the end of the Book of Judges, for example, the
aged Ephraimite, pleading with the vicious Benjaminites
bent on assaulting his Levite guest, says:

> "No, my brethren ... seeing that this man has come into
> my house, do not commit this criminal folly. Behold, here
> are my virgin daughter and his concubine; let me now
> bring them out. Rape them and do to them as seems best
> to you; but against this man do not commit the *dābhār* of
> this criminal folly." (Judges 19:23-24).

"The *dābhār* of this criminal folly" here clearly means something more and worse than the simpler "this criminal folly" of the preceding verse. As the second verse implies, the rape of the daughter and of the concubine is in the category of "this criminal folly (*han-nᵉbhālā haz-zōth*)": the assault upon the Levite is also in this category, but in his case it is something more and worse: it is the *dābhār* —the very essence ("word")—"of this criminal folly." The translations of the Revised Standard Version ("so vile a thing") and the New English Bible ("such an outrage") miss the force of the Hebrew *dābhār han-nᵉbhālā haz-zōth;* the old Ephraimite's plea requires some such rendering as "Do not commit the most quintessentially criminal kind there is of this criminal folly."

"Word" meaning "inner character" is also evident in the following passage:

> At the end of every seven years you shall grant a release.
> And the *dābhār* of the release: every creditor shall release
> ... (Deut. 15:1-2).

The "*dābhār* of the release" is the *character* of the release: what "release" essentially consists of, and how it is to be executed. Here are several additional examples of the usage: "... and they shall declare to you *the specific import* of the decision (*dᵉbhar ham-mishpāṭ*)," i.e., specifically what the decision entails, its *character* (Deut. 17:9); "... the kind of manslayer (*dᵉbhar hā-rōṣēªḥ*)" (Deut. 19:4); "...the *character* of the forced labor (*dᵉbhar ham-mas*)" (I Kings 9:15); and there are still other instances.

In ancient Israel, then, words were taken for granted to be the inner, specific characters of their respective realities. This point about the nature of words, so important to proper understanding of the theory and practice of literature in ancient Israel, is further corroborated by the usage in Biblical Hebrew of the main term for that class of words which consists of proper nouns, namely, "name" (*shēm*). "Name" in classical Hebrew does not mean merely the symbol whereby communication is achieved of reference to some person, group, class or locality. Like "word," "name" was thought of as integrally bound up with its referent; and again like "word," it means "essential character," though mainly, of course, with reference to human beings and other species of "soul."[7]

That person and name were regarded in ancient Israel as aspects of one and the same soul is frequently illustrated in the Scriptures. The name, as we see, is held to be the person, so that as long as the name remains among the living, the person too is present. That is why, for instance, we can be told that

> Absalom in his lifetime had taken and set up for himself the pillar which is in the King's Valley, for he said, "I have no son so as to keep my name in remembrance"; he called the pillar after his own name, and it is called Absalom's Monument to this day (II Samuel 18:18).

Absalom did this so that his name—he himself as such—might live on after his death. Every time someone said "Absalom's Monument," he would be present among the living in the form of his mentioned name; he would not have become utterly extinct. Complete destruction and extinction of personality, accordingly, is expressed as a "blotting-out," a "perishing," a "cutting-off" of the *name*. Several examples:

> And he will give their kings into your hand and you shall make their name perish from under heaven ...
> (Deut. 7:24);

> For the Canaanites and all the inhabitants of the land will ... cut off our name from the earth; and what wilt thou do regarding thine own great name? (Joshua 7:8);

> But the Lord had not given word to blot out the name of Israel from under heaven, so he delivered them ...
> (II Kings 14:27).

As indicated, "name" means "essential character" in the

---

[7] J. Barr, "The Symbolism of Names in the Old Testament" (*Bulletin of the John Rylands Library*, LII [1969-1970], 11-29), argues for a "symbolic" rather than an "integralist" interpretation by Abigail of her husband's name "Nabal" (I Sam. 25:25). But even if we accept Barr's view that "Nabal" in Biblical Hebrew was a homonym that could mean either something like "one sent (by God)" or "churlish fool," it does not follow that the name itself was not thought of as Nabal's "essential character"—indeed as Nabal's very person—and not just as a means of referring to him for some communicative purpose.

sense of a substantive identity whose special qualities and characteristics distinguish it and so enable it to be known and recognized. When Israel prays,

> But thou, O God, my Lord, act with me for thy name's sake (Ps. 109:21),

the petition is that the Lord act "in character," justly and mercifully. When Jeremiah says,

> There is none like thee, O Lord;
> thou art great,
> and thy name is great in might (10:6),

he is asserting that uniquely great power is a special characteristic of God. And when the Psalmist, offering thanks to God, says

> ... and I thank thy name for thy steadfast love and thy faithfulness; for thou hast made thy word great, above all thy name (Ps. 138:2),

he is expressing gratitude for the love and faithfulness of God's character which their consequence and reflex—the fulfillment of his promises—have shown to be preeminent in the hierarchy of the divine attributes.

Very important for "name" in the sense of "essential character"—for the significance, too, of "calling" or "pronouncing"—is the passage in which man is made partner with God in the creation of cattle, birds and beasts:

> So God formed out of the ground all the beasts of the field and all the birds of the skies, and brought (each) to the man to consider what he should call it, for all that the man would call "living soul"—that was to be its name. And then the man pronounced names for all the cattle, and for the birds of the skies, and for all the beasts of the field ... (Gen. 2:19-20).

Failure to take properly into account the ancient Israelite conception and usage of "name" that are central to this passage has resulted in the mistranslations of it which appear in our modern versions. The second half of 2:19 ("... for all that the man would call 'living soul'—that was to be its name") appears in the Revised Standard Version, the Modern Jewish Version, and the New English Bible, to specify only these, as "... and whatever the man called every (NEB: *each*) living creature, that was (MJV: *would be*) its name." In the Hebrew, however, the word "every" (*kol-*) does not appear immediately before "living creature" (*nephesh ḥayyā*) as, if these translations were correct, classical Hebrew grammar would require; and the fact that Hebrew syntax precludes the rendering "whatever the man called" is an additional reason to reject the translations as incorrect. More importantly, these mistranslations miss the main point of the passage: that man, whose own formation and vitality are directly given him by God (Gen. 2:7), has been permitted by God to bring the animal creation to life, and to endow the several main groupings of that creation with the attributes that distinctively characterize each. The man, as the passage states, by pronouncing the *name* "living soul" upon the animals and birds "formed out of the ground" and brought to him by God, first confers the general character of vitality upon them, and then, by pronouncing *names* for the cattle, birds and beasts, he endows them with the more specific characteristics which severally distinguish them. The passage thus presents man as participating with God in creating the vitality and the various natures of animals and birds; he is thus not only made dominant over this creation (cf. Gen. 9:1-3; Psalm 8), but given responsibility for its preservation and continued existence (hence Gen. 9:4). What God is to man in respect of the latter's vitality and essential nature, such, according to our passage, God has willed man to be with respect to the animal-and-bird creation. The method and instrumentalities used by man in performing these acts of creation, we note, are the very ones used by God Himself in creating other parts of the cosmos: He pronounces words that *name*, and so produce, the world's reality. As we are told in the summary account of the creation of man, given at Gen. 5:1-2, it is an act of divine *naming* that confers humanity upon both male and female:

> On the day of God's creating man, He made him in the semblance of God. Male and female did He create them, and He blessed them; and He pronounced their name "Man" on the day of their being created.

By the creators of the Hebrew Bible, words/names, the medium of literature, were, as the foregoing examples demonstrate, assumed to be entities of a concreteness and force that far transcend the quality and potency attributed to words and names in our modern western cultures. A word or name, in ancient Israelite perception seen as the concentrated form, or inner aspect, of its referent, was also held potentially capable—God permitting—of enacting such referent, of bringing it into being.

### 3. The Presumed Properties and Powers of Words

Implicit in the nature of words, as perceived in ancient Israel's culture, are the extra-communicative properties and powers which we must now notice. Here again, a word of caution: the properties and powers illustrated in the examples I am going to cite are not "just metaphors and similes," rhetorical and poetical devices employed for purposes of more effective communication and expression. In ancient Israel, owing to the conception of the nature of words, verbal and linguistic similarities and comparisons of every kind— metaphor, simile, paronomasia, and all other figures of diction—were held indicative of—indeed, constitutive of— relationships and effects not restricted, as in our modern cultures, to matters of communication and expression.

Since words were assumed to be compacted or concentrated forms of their referents, they could be thought of as possessing the properties of those referents. Where the referents are material, palpable, or otherwise sensible things or acts, the words are endowed with a concreteness that to the ancient Israelite was quite literally, and not—as with modern writers and readers—just metaphorically a quality of his poetry or prose. Thought of as palpable, material objects, as things made, achieved or done, words were regarded as sensibly perceptible, susceptible of being acted upon, movable and transformable.

It does not, for example, seem incongruous or paradoxical to ancient Israelite minds that words—unwritten utterances—may be referred to as visible:

"O generation, see for yourselves the word of the Lord"
(Jer. 2:31);

The word which Isaiah the son of Amoz saw concerning
Judah and Jerusalem (Isa. 2:1);

The word of the Lord which came to Micah of Moresheth
... which he saw concerning Samaria and Jerusalem
(Micah 1:1).

The fact that the Lord's word was considered not merely
audible but visible is manifested in a verse in which "word"
is the object of both "see" and "hear":

For which (false prophet) has stood in close enough inti-
macy with Lord to see and to hear His word? (Jer. 23:18).

The eating of words—hence the tasting of them—is not,
as in our American parlance, a matter of taking them back,
of not living up to them, but of quite literally taking them into
the bodily apparatus of the personality:

Thy words were found, and I ate them;
    and thy words became a joy to me,
    and the rejoicing of my heart ... (Jer. 15:16).

Ezekiel, obeying an injunction to eat a scroll inscribed with
"lamentations, moaning and woe," finds it "sweet as honey"
(Ezek. 2:10-3:3). "Pleasant words are a honeycomb, sweet to the
taste" (Prov. 16:24), whereas the "arrow" aimed by the wicked
is "a bitter word" (Ps. 64:4[3]). And Amos prophesies that a
time would come when the inhabitants of the land, hungering
and thirsting for hearing the words of the Lord, would rove
about seeking His word, but not find it (Amos 8:11-12).

Perceived as material objects, words can be declared
"brought" (Gen. 37:2), "sent forth" (Ps. 107:20), "taken away"
(Isa. 31:2), and "ridden" (Ps. 45:5[4]). They are compared
with, even asserted to be, various products, instruments,
natural phenomena:

His words were softer than oil, yet they were drawn
swords (Ps. 55:22);

Thy word is a lamp to my feet (Ps. 119:105);

> Is not thus my word: like a fire, declares the Lord, and like
> a rock-crushing hammer? (Jer. 23:29).

And it is because words are thought of as palpable substances that they can be said to be "put in the mouth" of some person (Exod. 4:15, II Sam. 14:3 and 19, Isa. 51:16, etc.).

When the referent is an event or course of events, an act, action or sequence of actions, "words" may be "done," or "(ful)filled," or "made to stand":

> "As for the word which you have spoken to us in the name
> of the Lord, we will not listen to you. But we shall indeed
> do the whole of the word which went forth from our
> mouths, to wit, burn incense to the queen of heaven and
> pour out libations to her ..." (Jer. 44:16-17);

> So Solomon expelled Abiathar from being priest to the
> Lord, filling the word of the Lord which He had spoken
> against the house of Eli in Shiloh (I Kings 2:27).

With the more literal translation "filling" rather than the better English "fulfilling," we here glimpse a further aspect of "word" as conceived in ancient Israel: that true or substantiated words are "full," untrue words are "empty." "My word," the Lord is quoted as saying, "... that which issues from my mouth ... shall not return to me empty, but it shall have accomplished what I desire, and shall have prospered that as to which I sent it" (Isa. 55:10-11). In both the foregoing examples, be it noted, the referent of "word" is a course of actions or of events. The referent of a "word" which the Lord is sworn "to make to arise"—i.e., to fulfill—is likewise a sequence of events: the dispossessing by the Israelites of the nations occupying the Promised Land (Deut. 9:5); the nuance in this instance is the causing of the word to rise from its concentrated essential state to its full stature and stance as actualized reality.

As indicated, words were not merely presumed to have the properties of material objects, but might be thought of as foci or concentrations of dynamic power. They were plainly regarded as not only movable but mobile, not only as susceptible to being acted upon, but capable of acting upon other entities in ways not confined to communication, of producing and enacting effects, conditions, circumstances and states.

The mobility of words comes to view in classical Hebrew usage when "word," or an equivalent, is subject of an intransitive verb of motion. Some of the many examples:

His (the Lord's) word runs swiftly (Ps. 147:15);

... And my words which I have put in your mouth shall not depart out of your mouth ... (Isa. 59:21);

By myself I have sworn,
    justice has gone forth from my mouth,
    a word, and it will not return,
that to me every knee shall bow,
    every tongue shall swear (Isa. 45:23);

Then Laban and Bethuel answered, "The word has gone forth from the Lord; we are unable to propose anything to you, bad or good. Behold, Rebekah is before you. Take her, and go, that she may be wife to your master's son, as the Lord has spoken" (Gen. 24:50-51).

The power of words to move, as well as to constitute the willed and spoken whole of created reality, is exhibited in the famous saying,

... that man cannot live by bread alone, but man will live by the whole of that which goes forth from the mouth of the Lord (Deut. 8:3).

The presumed capability of words to move also accounts for the formula, found over and over again in the Hebrew Scriptures: "the word of the Lord came to so-and-so." "Came" here is a form of the Hebrew verb hāyā, which means "to fall out, come to pass, come into being, become." Literally translated, the formula means "the word of the Lord came into being unto so-and-so," i.e., "so-and-so experienced (or: received) an incidence of the Lord's word."

The movement of a divine word to full realization is described as a "coming" of the word:

"... with the coming of the prophet's work, the prophet will be known as one whom the Lord has truly sent" (Jer. 28:9);

Until the time of the coming of His word, the Lord's statement tested him (Ps. 105:19).

Failure of a word to achieve or to maintain actualization
is termed a "falling" or a "not standing":

> Not a word has fallen of the whole of the good word which
> the Lord spoke unto the house of Israel: the whole has
> come (Josh. 21:45);

> Know then that no part of the word of the Lord which the
> Lord spoke unto the house of Ahab shall fall to the
> ground, since the Lord has now done that which He spoke
> by His servant Elijah (II Kings 10:10);

> Plot a plan, and it will be annulled, speak a word, and it
> will not stand, for God is with us (Isa. 8:10).

Our Biblical Hebrew texts frequently exemplify the
dynamic powers and capabilities attributed to words in
ancient Israel. Words, it was supposed, can kill: "... I have
slain them by the words of my mouth ..." (Hos. 6:5); or they
can create:

> By the word of the Lord were the heavens made, by the
> breath of His mouth all their host (Ps. 33:6);

> God said, "Let there be light," and there was light (Gen. 1:3);

> Fruit of lips is creating well-being (Isa. 57:19).

Because words were assumed to be invested with power,
words predicative of disaster were dreaded, and those
threatened, hearing them, might seek to arouse the divine
compassion by exhibiting signs of mourning. King Hezekiah,
hearing the threats of the Assyrian envoy, rent his garments
(II Kings 19:1), as did King Josiah when he learned the words
of the book of the Torah which had been found in the house
of the Lord (II Kings 22:11-13). Even when such words were
not believed, those who uttered them were considered so
subversive of the general welfare that they risked execution.
"You must die," Jeremiah is told by his hearers. "Why have
you prophesied in the Lord's name, saying ... 'this city shall
be a desolation without inhabitant'?" (Jer. 26:8-9). A divine
word was sometimes uttered to allay the misgivings caused
by the words of powerful men. Isaiah tells Hezekiah's servants:

> "You may say this to your master: 'Thus says the Lord: Do
> not be afraid of the words which you heard when the lads
> of the King of Assyria blasphemed me'" (II Kings 19:6).

And the Lord, referring to the brazen and obdurate folk to
whom He is sending Ezekiel, bids the prophet:

> ... do not be afraid of their words, nor be dismayed before
> them, for they are a rebellious house (Ezek. 2:6).

Very important for the perception of literature in ancient
Israel was the belief that words, formulated and asserted as
statements of what existent or actual persons, things and
circumstances are "like," could be enacted as—might come
to be—those very actualities. This assumption, doubtless
very ancient, underlies the various kinds of word-magic—
spells, charms and the like—found in most human societies
and cultures. The fact that this capability was believed in
ancient Israel to inhere in words is validated by many references in the Scriptures. Such a word-"likeness" is termed a
*māshāl* (frequently translated "proverb," "parable," "figure,"
etc.), its framer a *mōshēl* (plural *mōsheʟīm*), or a *memashshēl*. In
a *māshāl* directed "against the king of Babylon," for example,
the latter is met in the underworld by the shades of the dead
kings of the nations, who say to him,

> "You too have been made weak like us, unto us have you
> been likened" (Isa. 14:10).

"You have been likened" (*nimshaltā*) is here the synonymous
parallel to "you have been made weak like us." The declaration that the Babylonian king has been "likened" to the
shades of the dead kings is regarded as the equivalent of
producing in that (still alive and functioning) monarch the
actual weakness of the dead. When the Psalmist prays

> To thee, O Lord, I call out;
> O my Rock, be not too deaf for me,
> lest thou be too silent for me,
> and I be likened with those going down
>         to the Pit (Ps. 28:1),

the "likening" is deemed capable of making the indicated
descent the Psalmist's actuality, unless God should decree

otherwise; the same conception appears in another Psalm:

> Make haste, answer me, O Lord:
>> My spirit fails!
> Do not hide thy face from me,
>> Or I shall be likened
>>> with those going down to the Pit (Ps. 143:7).

Again, in the course of a lament over Jerusalem, the poet says:

> What witness can I bear of you,
>> to what can I declare you like,
>>> O daughter of Jerusalem?
> What can I liken to you,
>> that I may relieve you,
>>> O virgin daughter of Zion?
> For great as the sea is your fracture:
> Who will heal you? (Lam. 2:13).

"Declare ... like" (dāmā, intensive form) and "liken" here are
considered capable of effecting the relieving of Jerusalem's
plight, the healing of its fractured state. And when God is
represented as asking,

> Whom would you make me resemble,
>> Or make me like?
>> Or liken me,
> that we be alike? (Isa. 46:5, cf. 40:19, 25),

the questions both assert the divine uniqueness, and,
denying that man can make ("liken") what is truly God,
expose idol-making and idolatry as arrant folly.

### 4. "Holy Words"

The most powerful of all words, as the creators of the
Hebrew Scriptures perceived the medium of literature, were
"holy words," words believed to have been uttered by God
Himself, whether directly, as in the creation of the world, or
more commonly indirectly, "at the mouth of" prophets.
Hearing such words, speaking or reading them out, or
writing them down meant coming into physical contact with
aggregates of enormous power. We have the following
descriptions, by the prophet Jeremiah, of how contact with
some of the Lord's "holy words" affected him:

> My heart within me is broken,
>     all my bones shake;
> I am like a drunkard,
>     like a man overcome by wine,
> Because of the Lord,
>     and because of his holy words (Jer. 23:9);

> ... the Lord's word has become for me a derision and a
> shame all the time. But should I say, "I will not mention it,
> nor speak again in His name," then it is like a burning fire
> in my heart; if shut up in my bones, then I weary of holding
> it in, and cannot (Jer. 20:8-9).

No matter how well-intentioned or accidental, contact with a holy instrumentality by one not in condition to absorb the resultant inflow of power—as shown by the example of Uzziah son of Aminadab, who touched the ark of God at the threshing-floor of Nacon (II Samuel 6:6-7; I Chr. 13:9-10)— might be perilous and disruptive to the person thus in contact. In this respect, holy words were not considered essentially different from other vehicles, instrumentalities and appurtenances of holiness: they might be productive of health and welfare, or they could induce weakness and destruction. Holy words, accordingly, were to be handled quite as cautiously, circumspectly and reverently as was any object deemed freighted with divine power. And the evidence of our Scriptural texts shows the ever-present awareness of the composers and editors that such must be their *modus operandi* with aggregates of divine utterances.[8]

Of all holy words the holiest, of course, were the name and the various other designations of the Lord Himself. Although the nomenclature of the divine was not always subject to the circumlocutions and avoidances of later Jewish practice, the Scriptural use of such devices as euphemism in pejorative statements about God is plainly very ancient. When, for example, Job's wife advises her afflicted spouse,

> "Curse God and die" (Job 2:9),

the Hebrew word *bārēkh*, "bless," is what is written in the text, not one of the several words for "curse." The reader or

---

[8] See Chapter Four below.

hearer would, of course, understand from the context that
"curse" was the word intended, but the danger in pronouncing it would have been avoided, indeed guarded against and
off-set, by uttering "bless" instead. The narrative of Naboth's
judicial murder on the false charge of having *"cursed* God and
the king" (I Kings 21:10-13) exhibits the same euphemism; so
too the Psalmist's statement that "one seeking unjust gain has
*cursed,* has spurned the Lord" (Ps. 10:3).

Where grammatical or syntactic construction of the text
negates or qualifies the pejorative utterance, expressions
involving the execration of God do occur:

> You shall not revile God, nor curse a leader among your
> people (Exod. 22:27[28]);

> Each man, should he curse his God, must bear his sin (Lev.
> 24:15).

Since "spurning," as shown by the foregoing citation of Ps.
10:3—other instances occur at Num. 16:30, Isa. 1:4 and Ps.
74:10 ("your name")—could be used without euphemism in
speaking of God, the circumlocution employed by the
prophet Nathan in attributing an act of such "spurning" to
King David is all the more striking. Rebuking David for his
adultery-induced murder of Uriah the Hittite, Nathan
avoids saying aloud and openly that David has altogether
"spurned" the Lord, but says instead that David has altogether "spurned" 'the enemies of' the Lord (II Samuel 12:14).
That the surrogate for "the Lord" should be expressed in the
form of the enemies of the Lord here discloses the conviction
and presumption that underlie the rhetorical usage.
"Spurning"—slighting, deriding, exhibiting contempt of
someone—is something that might not safely be done to the
Lord, but could certainly be done with impunity to the
Lord's enemies. It might endanger the king if the prophet,
coming to him with the Lord's word, were to accuse him
outright of spurning the Lord. The charges of "spurning the
Lord" might properly be leveled against the wicked who
would deservedly be assailed by the Lord's wrath that might
thus be aroused, but not against those whom one would shield
from the noxious effects of that wrath.

The awe inspired by the Lord's holy words, and the necessity to handle these aggregates of divine power with concern for the security and weal of those who might come into contact with them underlie, and are evident in, the following instructions regarding prophets and the divine words sent through them into the world:

> "And the Lord said to me [Moses]: '... I will raise up for them a prophet from among their brethren like yourself; and I will put my words in his mouth, and he shall utter unto them all that I command him. As for the man who will not pay attention to my words which he will utter in my name, I myself will thereafter hold him accountable for this. But the prophet who presumes to utter a word in my name, that which I did not command him to utter, or who makes utterance in the name of other gods—then that prophet shall die.' Now should you be saying in your heart, 'How may we know the word which the Lord has not uttered?'—that which the prophet utters in the name of the Lord, and the word neither comes to pass not enters in, that is the word which the Lord has not uttered. With presumption did the prophet utter it: you shall not stand in awe of it" (Deut. 18:17-22).

A problem is adumbrated in the latter portion of this passage: how is covenant-loyal Israel to handle an unfulfilled word uttered in the name of the Lord by one known to have been a prophet of the Lord who has now died? Was the divine word uttered "presumptuously," was it a word that the Lord had not commanded him to utter, and had the prophet died because he had uttered it? Or was it in fact a word which the Lord did command him to introduce into the world, and was his death due to some other cause than his utterance of this word? If the word was a genuine divine word, it had to be handled and heeded as a holy word, an emergent creation of God. If it was not a genuine divine word, then such heeding and handling as were reserved for holy words were categorically forbidden. In view of Israel's direct accountability to the Lord for failure to heed his word, ability to distinguish a genuine divine utterance from a spurious one was a matter of life-and-death importance. Hence the question: "How may we know the word which the Lord has not uttered?" The answer: if and when the word comes fully to be part of the world's reality, you will recognize it as genuinely a word uttered by the Lord. Now the interval between initial utterance and full actualization might, of course, be a long one, but until such time as it might become obvious that the word was not going to be fully actualized, it was to be regarded and handled as if it were a genuine utterance of the Lord's: it was to be regarded with awe and handled with circumspect care. Once, however, it was evident that the prophet had spoken "presumptuously,"—that this particular word would never be actualized—then to regard and handle it as if it were a "holy word" of the Lord's was expressly forbidden: "you shall not stand in awe of it." Most of our modern English translations of this passage make the final pronoun "him" rather than "it" (Hebrew does not distinguish a neuter pronoun); they make the prophet, not the presumptuously spoken word, that of which the Israelites are forbidden to stand in awe. Since, however, the prophet involved is one who is already dead, to forbid standing in awe of him is nugatory, if not absurd; the pronoun's antecedent, both grammatically and logically, can only be "word," not "prophet." The mistranslations illustrate how difficult it is for persons brought up in a modern western culture to grasp statements involving such different beliefs about the nature and power of words as those of ancient Israel.

As will be shown in a later chapter, editorial caution in the handling of "holy words" has had two important textual consequences. It has, in the first place, been a main factor in bringing the prophetic materials of our Scriptural books of literary prophecy into their present order and sequence—or rather, from the standpoint of any reader brought up in modern western culture, into their present disorder and confused disposition. Secondly, it is ultimately responsible for the textual conflation so abundantly in evidence throughout the Hebrew Bible. "Holy words," of course, are special in point of power and capability, and it is only to be expected that some of the "strangest" and most startling textual and literary phenomena in the Scriptures are consequences of what the ancient Israelites believed about such words.

Not only these phenomena, however, but all the textual and rhetorical operations, usages and devices that confront us in the Hebrew Bible spring from, are conditioned and influenced by, what the producers of those Scriptures took for granted about words, both human and divine—what they assumed words to be, how they presumed them to behave, what they considered them able to do.

# CHAPTER TWO

## ANCIENT ISRAEL'S BELIEFS
## ABOUT THE LITERARY PROCESS

The matter and manner of Biblical Hebrew literature are defined not only by the ancient Israelite assumptions regarding the nature and powers of words as such, but by that culture's assumptions about the writing down and the reading of bodies of ordered words, of texts. It may not simply be taken for granted that the cultural postulates of modern western societies governing the production and reading of literary works are equally valid for the culture of ancient Israel. The difference in this respect between a modern western society and ancient Israel does not extend merely to the physical book and to the circumstances and techniques involved in its manufacture and distribution,[9] but equally, if not more, to the culturally defined circumstances in which works of literary art are written and read. In a modern western society, for example, it is normally expected that the author or compiler of a literary work will be identified and known by name. In ancient Israel, on the contrary, except for one book of the Apocrypha—Ecclesiasticus, or the Wisdom of Ben Sira—the authorship of no work of classical Hebrew or Aramaic literature that has come down to us is certainly known. By our western conventions, again, the reading of a literary text is something a person more often does in his solitariness than in association with others: while reading aloud to others does, of course, occur, when we think of "reader" we usually envisage them as persons engaged, separately and individually, in silently perusing a copy of some written literary composition. The reading of a literary text in ancient

---

[9] Cf. the article by D. J. Wiseman, "Books in the Ancient Near East and in the Old Testament," in *The Cambridge History of the Bible* I (Cambridge, 1970), 30-48.

Israel, on the other hand, was generally and typically a speech-act, always done aloud, and designed to accomplish certain effects in the phenomenal world—effects not necessarily confined to the readers and hearers of the text. So far as I am aware, nowhere in ancient Israel's Scriptures is there reference to a person sitting down and reading a book of verse or of fiction silently to himself for his own private delectation, as we commonly do today. Now the theory and practice of the literary art in a given society will be intimately bound up with, shaped and conditioned by, that society's culturally received and transmitted conventions as to composition, writing and reading. A grasp of ancient Israel's quite different cultural assumptions respecting these activities is therefore indispensable to genuine understanding of the literature before us in the Hebrew Bible. To retrieve these assumptions, now for the most part implicit in the contexts which allude to them, is the main purpose of this chapter.

## 1. Literacy

Judging by the fairly ample Biblical evidence, literacy was never an exceptional skill among the ancient Israelites. In the Gideon-story, for example, we are told that a boy from Succoth, caught by Gideon, "wrote down for him the officials and leading citizens of Succoth, seventy-seven men" (Judges 8:14); the narrative thus implies that literacy was a skill that any ordinary lad of such a town as pre-monarchy Succoth might be presumed to have. Again, the witnesses of Jeremiah's purchase of the field at Anathoth are described as "those writing (their names) in the deed of purchase" (Jer. 32:12). At the time of this transaction, Jeremiah was imprisoned "in the court of the guard," so that the witnesses had to chose from among those Judeans who happened to be there. The ready availability, among this relatively restricted group, of witnesses capable of signing the purchase-deed is indicative of a considerable incidence of literacy at Jerusalem during this time (ca. 587 B.C.E.).

Illiteracy, on the other hand, although it too must have been fairly common in all periods of Israel's history, is far less well attested in our Biblical Hebrew texts. A clear allusion to it is found, if I am not mistaken, only in the following passage:

> But the vision of the entire world-order has become for
> you like the words of the sealed copy of a deed: as to
> which, should people give it to him who knows letters and
> say, "Please read this," he will say "I cannot, for it is
> sealed." Or should they give the deed to one who does not
> know letters and say, "Please read this," he will say, "I do
> not know letters" (Isa. 29:11-12).

Even here, we note, the presumption is rather of literacy than
of illiteracy. Those who ask the man ignorant of letters to
read the document are represented as naturally expecting
him to have this skill. Noteworthy, too, is the fact that such
ignorance, if regarded as surprising, is evidently not so
socially censurable that a man might be reluctant to admit it.

Whatever may have been the statistical facts regarding
literacy and illiteracy in the historical actuality of ancient
Israel, the Israel envisaged in the Scriptures as the holy
creation of God was required to be a literate society. While
there is no specific commandment enjoining literacy as such,
each individual Israelite is made responsible for the fulfillment of religious obligations that require him either to write
himself, or else have others do his writing for him. Thus, of
the words of the commandment to love God with all his
heart, soul and might, the Israelite is told:

> "And you shall write them on the doorposts of your house
> and on your gates" (Deut. 6:9).

As required by divine injunction, again, the Israelite divorc-
ing his wife

> "... writes her a bill of divorce, puts it in her hand, and
> sends her away from his house ..." (Deut. 24:1).

And one particular Israelite—the king—has the obligation to

> "... write him the duplicate of this Torah according to a
> text issuing from the keeping of the Levitical priests ..."
> (Deut. 17:18).

The language of these injunctions might lead one to suppose
that the Israelite was to do the writing involved with his own
hand. That such is not the case, however, is shown by the

usage of "write" in the famous account of Jeremiah's scroll:
Jeremiah, commanded by the Lord to "take a scroll and write
on it all the words that I have spoken to you ...," calls Baruch
the son of Neriah, who, at Jeremiah's dictation writes down
all the words that had originally been spoken to the prophet
by the Lord (Jer. 36:1-4). As a divine command, then, "write"
signifies "get into writing," whether by one's own hand or
by that of somebody else. Judging by the many references to
them in the Scriptures, numerous trained, professional
scribes—the "ready scribe" of Psalm 45:2(1) and Ezra 7:6—
were at all times to be found in Israel, as in all the other literate cultures and civilizations of the ancient Near East; and
these could be counted upon to supply such requisite docu-
mentary expertise as the individual Israelite might lack.
Accordingly, acts involving literacy were to be obligatory
upon every Israelite, though he himself was not necessarily
required to be literate. While no particular opprobrium may
have historically attached to an individual unfamiliar with
letters, as suggested by Isa. 29:11-12, the producers of the Scriptures manifestly believed that the Israel of God's intention must be
a society deeply and irrevocably committed to literacy.

## 2. "Reading"

For the cultural postulation of "reading" in ancient
Israel, it is important to understand that qārā',the commonest
verb for "to read" in classical Hebrew, also signifies "call,"
"proclaim," "exclaim," "cry out" and various other nuances
of the action of producing meaningful sounds and voiced
words. "Reading," that is to say, was culturally assumed to
be an activity in which one pronounced ordered words
aloud. This assumption about reading figures, for example,
in a promise of future felicity:

> "The deaf on that day shall hear the words of a book, and,
> done with gloom and darkness, the eyes of the blind shall
> see" (Isa. 29:18).

The phenomenon of "silent reading" was probably not known
in ancient Israel. Even the "meditation" upon (literally "in")
written ordered words, enjoined by the Lord upon Joshua,—

"This book of the Torah shall not depart out of your
mouth, but you shall meditate upon it day and night, that
you be careful to act according to all that is written in it ..."
(Josh. 1:8).

—is expressed by a form of the verb *hāghā*, which may vari-
ously mean "utter," "growl," "moan." Accordingly, when we
are told that

Hezekiah took the documents from the messengers and
read them ... (II Kings 19:14),

or that Shaphan "read" the "book of the Torah" found by the
high priest Hilkiah in the House of the Lord (II Kings 22:8),
the presumption must be that the reading was done aloud.
And we must understand the injunction upon the king to read
in "the copy of this Torah ... all the days of his life" (Deut.
17:18-19) to mean that he must either read it aloud himself
or have it read out in his hearing; as shown by the context of
II Kings 22:16, "read" may mean "have (a text) read out," just
as "write" may mean "get into writing" (see above).

The fact that "reading" in ancient Israel always signified
the use of the voice in pronouncing ordered words has at
least two important corollaries. First, it is plain that in this
culture "reading" was not as correlative of "writing" as it is
in our western culture. When, for example, in the narrative
of the prophecy against the altar at Bethel, it is said that the
"man of God ... pronounced against the altar the word of the
Lord ..." (I Kings 13:2), the Hebrew here might also be translated "... read out against the altar the word of the Lord": the
ambiguity and the translation-option exist because we do not
know whether the "word" which the man of God brought
from Judah to Bethel was, or was not, a written word.
Second, it may not be excluded that words other than *qārā'*
were used to indicate what in western culture would be
termed "reading," since there are other verbs in classical
Hebrew which express various nuances of the use of voice
in connection with ordered words, written or unwritten.
Thus, for example, the "declaring" (*higgīdh*) and the "answer-
ing and saying" (*'ānā we'āmar*) involved in the first-fruits

liturgy described in Deut. 26:1-11 may imply the recitation
of a set text, possibly a written text. Mention should here be
made, too, of the frequently found idiomatic uses of the verb
*nāsā'* "to lift up," "carry," "take up"; the word "voice" is
often the direct object of this verb, as

> The voice of your watchmen!
> They have lifted voice,
>     together they shout for joy! (Isa. 52:8);

> And Esau lifted up his voice and wept (Gen. 28:38).

Instead of "voice" the "lifting-up" may have for object the
word *māshāl*, which, as pointed out above, basically means
a "likening-through-words," and, in our translations, is vari-
ously rendered "proverb" (e.g., "The proverbs of Solomon ..."
[Prov. 1:1]), "parable," "similitude":

> And Balaam lifted up his parable, and said ... (Num. 23:7,
> 18; 24:3, 15, 20, 21, 23);

> And you shall lift up this similitude against the king of
> Babylon, and say ... (Isa. 14:4);

> And Job again lifted up his parable and said ... (Job 27:1).

Other such grammatical objects of the verb *nāsā'* "lift up" are:
*tephillā* "prayer" (II Kings 9:4; Jer. 7:16); *qīnā* "elegy," "lamentation" (Jer. 7:29; Amos 5:1); and very frequently the cognate
noun *massā'* "oracle," "burden," (Isa. 13:1; 15:1; Jer. 23:36, 38;
Ezek. 12:10; Nahum 1:1; Zech. 9:1, etc.). All of these, we note,
are *compositions* of ordered words. It was because each such
composition was *assumed to be voiced aloud*, possibly in a
specially formal manner, that it could form the object of the
verb "lift up"; "And they will lift up a lamentation over you
..." (Ezek. 26:17) means "they will lift up (their voices in
mournfully pronouncing) a lamentation over you ..." Each
such word-composition, that is, in terms of its idiomatic
usage with the verb *nāsā'* was a variant of "voice" in the
expression "to lift up (one's) voice."

It follows, then, that in ancient Israel's culture the normal
correlative of reading, or of both reading and writing, was
*composition*, the production of ordered words. All composition
was designed to be "read," in the sense of to be pronounced

aloud, but not all that was composed and "read" was necessarily written; all that was written was, of course, designed to be read by somebody at some time or other subsequent to the composition and the writing. Literary compositions were only written down if intended to serve a purpose that could alone be achieved through such a writing down. For instance, songs like those mentioned in the composition referred to as "The Harlot's Song"—

> "Get a harp
> go round the town,
> O harlot to be forgotten!
> Make your music sweet,
> make your songs many,
> that you may be remembered" (Isa. 23:15-16)

—were certainly compositions designed for *viva voce* presentation, but it is extremely doubtful if they were written. Indeed, except for the fact that these lines of satiric verse are quoted in a prophecy against Tyre, which *was* written down, we should probably not have known that there ever was such a composition as the Harlot's Song. Similar instances are Jotham's *māshāl* or parable (Judges 9:7-21) and the verses of the taunt against Moab, which, we are told, "the *mōshᵉlīm*"— the makers of word-likenesses—"were saying" (Numbers 21:27-30). Although these compositions, and others like them, were unquestionably made in order to be pronounced, it is doubtful if their authors originally put them into writing. Their presence now in a written text is the result of considerations quite different from this that initially led to their production.

From Jeremiah 51:59-64 (to be more fully discussed below), as well as from Jeremiah 36 and many other passages, it is clear that the reading-out of a written text of ordered words was thought of as made possible by, but not necessarily as constituting the main purpose of, their original composition and recording. There is of course, a difference between the purpose served by the reading-out in the case of the passage in Jeremiah 51 and the purpose of the reading about which we are told in Jeremiah 36: whereas in the latter the stated purpose is the quasi-communicative one of making it possible for the Judeans to repent, and so for the Lord to forgive their sins (Jer. 36:3), in the former the purpose served is the quasi-magical triggering of full realization of the doom upon Babylon. The narrative about the writing of the *second* scroll in Jeremiah 36 (vv. 27-32), which, in contrast to the story about the first scroll (vv. 2-26), makes no mention at all of any reading of it, is a further indication that the purpose of writing down the Lord's words was not necessarily, or solely, the communication of those words to as large an audience or readership as possible. Plainly, according to the accounts of both Jeremiah 51 and Jeremiah 36, the original purpose of the Lord's uttering his words was conceived of as something far transcending any use to which the recorded form of those words might be put, while the reading-out of the written words was an act believed capable of effects not merely confined to those obtainable through communication and expression.

Examples will be cited in the next chapter of the extraordinary fact that the reading-out of ordered words might be addressed to an absent, or an unwitting, person or human group, or even to an insentient object or locale. *Māshāls*, again, like those "lifted" by Balaam upon Israel (Numbers 22-24), while considered more efficacious if pronounced within sight of the intended recipients of the impact of the words, did not necessarily have to be heard by the recipients. Divine words, on the other hand, if they involved action dependent upon the recipients' volition, did require physical audition, and were recorded to facilitate repetitions of such audition. Written or unwritten, however, a composition of ordered words, if "read," was culturally postulated in ancient Israel as a launching (or a relaunching) of those words into the world—of words whose nature and powers, as taken for granted in that culture, were those described in Chapter One above.

## 3. "Writing"

Equally with the spoken word, the ancient Israelites considered the written word as intrinsically and necessarily connected with its "real" referent, indeed as being the "real"

referent in this particular form.[10] This assumption figures in
the narrative, told in Numbers, of how 70 of the leading men
among Israel received from the Lord a portion of the "spirit
upon Moses" that they might help him "bear the burden of
the people" (Num. 11:17). This conferring of a portion of the
spirit upon the 70, whose names were written down in a list,
was to be done outside the Camp, at the Tent of meeting (vv.
16, 24). "Now two men" the narrative continues,

> stayed behind in the camp, one named Eldad, the second
> Medad; but as they were among those written, the spirit
> rested upon them even though they had not gone out to
> the Tent; so they were prophetically possessed within the
> Camp. Thereupon a lad ran and told Moses, and said, "Eldad
> and Medad are showing themselves as prophets within
> the Camp!" At this, Joshua son of Nun, Moses' chosen ser-
> vant, spoke up and said, "My Lord Moses, stop them!" But
> Moses said to him, "Are you jealous on my behalf? Rather
> would that all the Lord's people were prophets, that the Lord
> would set his spirit upon them" (Num. 11:26-29).

Here we find that the *written names* were sufficiently in themselves the human realities, the actual personalities, to make
manifest in them the identical physical effects of the accession
of the spirit that they presumably would have exhibited had
they, like their 68 colleagues, left the Camp and been stationed
close to the Tent. The *written names* are here shown to be the
persons themselves in this particular aspect of their being.

The same assumption—that the written terms are the
inscriptional form, as it were, of their actual referents—also
figures in the account of Joshua's assignment of portions of
the land to the seven tribes whose territories were as yet not
specified:

> Accordingly, Joshua said to the Israelites, "... Assign three
> men per tribe ... that they may set out, travel through the coun-
> try, and write it down according as each (tribe) might have
> a heritage ... You yourselves will thus write the land in
> seven divisions, and bring it to me here; and I will cast a
> lot for you here before the Lord our God ..." So off the men
> went: they traversed the land, and they wrote it by cities,
> by seven divisions, upon a book; then they came to the

---

[10] Cf. II Samuel 18:18, discussed in Chapter One, above.

> Camp at Shiloh. And Joshua cast a lot for them in Shiloh
> before the Lord; there Joshua apportioned the land to the
> Israelites according to their divisions (Josh. 18:3-10).

As the wording of the passage shows, the "book" upon
which the land was written "by cities, by seven divisions,"
is here regarded as the actual land itself, trimmed into a form
that made it able to be brought to Joshua and to be assignable
by lot to the seven tribes. Judging by the remainder of the
account in Joshua 18-19, the "apportioning" was presumably
done as follows: one of the "written divisions" was first *read
out*, and thus the actual territory, in the form of the
pronounced names of the cities and the pronounced words
tracing the boundaries, was placed before all the interested
parties. Then, from a container holding seven distinguish-
able lots, one for each tribe, there was a casting, and the territory so written and pronounced was assigned to the tribe
whose lot "came out"; the tribe was held to have been given
the actual territory, and not merely the written (and
pronounced) description of the territory.

Ezekiel, again, is directed to

> "... propound the House to the house of Israel, that they
> may be ashamed of their iniquities, and let them take its
> measure. And ... make known to them and write down, as
> they look on, the delineation of the House; its interior, ex-
> its, entrances, and its entire form, together with all its stat-
> utes—the whole of its lineaments and of its revealed
> procedures—that they may observe the whole of its delinea-
> tion and all its statutes, and enact them" (Ezek. 43:10-11).

The future Temple, with all its physical features, appurtenances and procedures is thus directly *experienced in this written form* by the representatives of the Israel upon whose volition and action its divinely ordained building and use
depend.

It is this same conception of the written word as the
"real" referent in this form—the real entity, phenomenon or
event, present or future or both—that makes it possible to
speak of "writers who write oppression" (Isa. 10:1); or to say
to people, respecting a Judean king,

"Write this man down as childless, a man unsuccessful in
his days" (Jer. 22:30);

or to pray that kings and nobles be clapped into irons,

"to execute against them the judgment written" (Ps.
149:9).

The "book which thou hast written" from which Moses prays
to be "blotted out" if the Lord will not forgive the people's
sin of idolatry (Exod. 32:32), is plainly the entire future
world, including all the persons who are to constitute the
population of that world, as designed by God and, in written
form, thought of as present with him. This "book" also
figures in the Lord's reply to Moses:

"Whoever has sinned respecting me, him will I blot out
from my book" (*ibid.* v. 33).

If the Psalmist can pray that his enemies,

... be blotted out of the book of those to live, and not be
written along with the righteous (Ps. 69:29[28]),

it is because to be "written" in that "book" is already the
created actuality of human salvation.

*4. "Book"*

The classical Hebrew word for the important term
"book" is *sēpher*. As used, the word designates "list," "letter"
(in the sense of a missive), "inscription" and "document."
Even more significantly for our purposes, as we saw above
in the citation of Isa. 29:12, it is a collective noun used in the
sense of "letter"; so too at Daniel 1:3-4:

Then the king commanded Ashpenaz, his chief eunuch, to
enlist some Israelites of the royal line and of the nobility,
youths ... capable of holding a position in the King's pal-
ace, and to have them taught letters [*sēpher*; NEB: litera-
ture] and the Chaldaean language.

As in Greek the term for "letters," *grammata*, and in Latin,
*literae*, so *sēpher* is the nearest classical Hebrew equivalent for
our modern term "literature." It will, accordingly, be useful to
try to glimpse the essential meaning of this key-term, that

which underlies the several disparate senses in which it is used in our Biblical Hebrew texts.

*Sāphar*, the verb most closely cognate with the noun-form *sēpher*, has the basic sense of "to count," "to tally"; this fact— that the noun which designates "book," "letters," "litera- ture," etc. is formed on a verbal stem meaning "to count"—is a clue to the ancient Israelite manner of conceiving that noun. In the cultural consciousness of ancient Israel, that is to say, the act of "counting" and the artifacts and activities denoted by *sēpher* were assumed to be conceptually and actually related. As felt by the ancient Israelites, apparently, the point of relationship between *sēpher* and *sāphar*—between "piece(s)- of-writing" (="book," "letters," etc.) and "to count" —was the making of a significant *countable* mark upon some surface capable of registering such a mark, a surface from which, in turn, it could be read off again (=*qārā'*) or "recounted" (=*sippēr*, intensive form of *sāphar* "count"). If, for example, one wishes to find out the precise numbers or sum of the units that comprise a series or congeries, a natural way of accomplishing this is to set a mark representing each such unit upon some handy surface, and then to count up the number of marks. That the ancient Israelites were familiar with, and practiced, this technique is no mere speculation: the fact is attested by a passage of the Book of Joshua, where the curious wording and arrangement are plainly the conse- quences of making a count in just this way:

> And these are the kings of the land whom Joshua and the Israelites smote on the westward side of the Jordan ... :

| | |
|---|---|
| the king of Jericho | one; |
| the king of Ai-beside-bethel | one; |
| the king of Jerusalem | one; |
| Totality of kings: | thirty-one (Josh. 12:7-24). |

Here the word "one" which follows the name of each of the thirty-one kings in the congeries was originally a *mark*, doubtless the perpendicular stroke found in ancient Hebrew and Aramaic inscriptions which signifies the numeral "1." When, subsequently, there was occasion to *read out* this list- ing—as, for example, in dictating it to a scribe—each such mark was necessarily *pronounced* as the word "one" *'eḥādh*; and so, in the textual transmission of the list the spelled-out word, as pronounced, came to be written out instead of the mark as set down on whatever writing-surface was originally used for the tally. It is in a counting-procedure of the kind attested by this passage, at any rate, that the felt point of relationship between *sāphar* and *sēpher* emerges clearly into view: *sāphar* is the classical Hebrew verb for the *act* of making a tally or count, while *sēpher* is the word for the material body of the resultant *tally*, the *surface* on or in which the count has been *marked off*. In whatever classical Hebrew context our word *sēpher* is found, and in whichever of its plurality of senses it may be used, it always continues to possess this connotation or nuance of a *surface on* which, or *within* the area of which, *meaningful marks* of some kind have been made.

That such is the case—that *sēpher* always connotes a surface that exhibits the effect of some meaningful or purposive marking, inscribing, or writing—is a point of considerable importance for the understanding of the languages and rhetoric of literary references in classical Hebrew, and indeed for the entire matter of the cultural postulation of literature in ancient Israel. If, for example, "book" (*sēpher*) and "tablet" (*lūᵃḥ*) can be used as synonymously parallel terms at Isaiah 30:8, this is because both terms connote *surface* "on" or "upon" which—both are objects of the preposition which expresses "on" in Hebrew (*'al*)—an indictment may be inscribed. Again, because *sēpher* is never without this connotation of "script-surface," where in English we may say only "in the book," in classical Hebrew "upon the book" is not only also permissible, but actually preferred. Thus, in all the many occurrences in Kings and in Chronicles of the formula, "... written in the Book of the Chronicles of the Kings of Israel/Judah," the Hebrew preposition is "upon" (*'al*), not "in" (*bᵉ-*). The nuance of slight distinction between "in (*bᵉ-*) the book" and "upon (*'al*) the book" and "upon (*'al*) the book" (where "in" would be required in English) seems to be that the former implies the place *in which* something previously said or written is now to be found, the latter the place *onto which* the writing-down of something was done; e.g.:

> ... as is written in (*bᵉ*-) the book of the Torah of Moses: "an altar of unhewn stones ..." (Josh. 8:31),

but

> "Is not that written in (*'al*) The Book of the Upright?" (Josh. 10:13).

The "surface"-connotation of *sēpher* also explains the fact that "from," in,

> "Seek and read from the Book of the Lord" (Isa. 34:16),

is in the Hebrew original literally "from-upon" (*mē 'al*); and so too, the usage of the same double preposition in the verse which tells us that

> Micaiah ... heard all the words of the Lord from the scroll (*mē 'al has-sēpher*) (Jer. 36:11).

Nearly synonymous with *sēpher* over the full range of its senses is *kᵉthābh*, whose basic meaning is "writing"; thus it means "register," "enrollment" (Ezek. 13:9, Ezra 2:62), "letter-character," "lettering," "alphabet" (Ezra 4:7, Esther 1:22), "missive," "letter" (II Chr. 2:10), "edict," "royal order" (II Chr. 35:4, Esther 3:14), and "book" (Daniel 10:21). But while both *sēpher* and *kᵉthābh* mean "book," if you are thinking of "book" chiefly as a "writing" you say *kᵉthābh*, whereas if you are thinking of "book" as an artifact that contains, or upon which is set out, a written grouping of composed words, you say *sēpher*.

In view of what has already been said of the relationship thought to obtain between a word and its phenomenal referent, it is readily apparent that the ancient Israelites perceived the relation between a book and its contents—its words—to be the same as that between a physical space or place and the phenomena and actions contained or carried on therein. It is because a book, or book-scroll, was commonly regarded as containing realities in their concentrated word-forms that it is possible for the prophet-poet to say,

> All the host of heaven shall dwindle away,
>    and the heavens shall be rolled up like a book (Isa. 34:4).

This view of the relation between a book and its contents

made its contribution, as we shall see, to the assembling of the Hebrew Scriptures.

*5. Literary Witness*

Closely allied to the postulation of the written words as inscribed variables of existent or future realities is the assumption that writing fixes, preserves, renders permanent what otherwise might be changeable, evanescent, impermanent. To say, for example, that "the sin of Judah is written with iron pen" (Jer. 17:1) emphasizes that Judah's sin is now to be regarded as a fixed circumstance, the penalty for which will inevitably be exacted; as "written"—even more indelibly, as graven with "iron pen"—that sin may no longer be considered a merely temporary, hence venial, lapse. So, too, when Job exclaims,

> "Oh that my words were written!
> Oh that they were inscribed in a book!
>     that with iron pen and lead
>     they were graven in the rock forever!" (Job 19:23-24),

he is expressing the wish that his claims, if unsatisfied, persist and last forever. In ancient Israel, to be "written down for life" implies continued vitality and effectiveness:

> It will come to pass that he that is left in Zion, and he that remains in Jerusalem, shall be termed holy, every one that is written down for life in Jerusalem (Isa. 4:3).

By the same token, written curses are curses permanently in effect: "... the curses written in this book" (Deut. 29:19[20]) will inevitably "settle down upon" the covenanted Israelite who persists in idolatry, "and the Lord will blot out his name from under heaven." Accordingly, it was to maintain their effectiveness and force, not merely to record them for future reference, that covenants, laws, contracts and rituals were practically always put into writing. And so too, incidentally, genealogies, since the persons named were thus kept "present" among the living.

A corollary of the cultural assumption just pointed out— that to put them in writing enables previously encountered life-experiences, arrangements and relationships to persist in continuing present and future significance—is of great importance for the perception of literature in ancient Israel. This is the belief that texts—groupings of written words—can, in and of themselves, attest, testify, perform the office of living witnesses: such word-groupings can warrant, acknowledge, give evidence, and constitute demonstration that such-and-such fact, condition or circumstance was, is, or will be really the case.

It will help us to appreciate the testatory powers attributed to groupings of written words in ancient Israel if we note that other artifacts and natural phenomena were also held capable of performing the office of a living witness. A heap of stones, for example, was to be witness of the covenant made by Laban and Jacob. The name "Heap of Witness" given it in both Aramaic and Hebrew by the two men established its function, and this could be deemed operative because the stones in fact, being God's handiwork and permanent, are a surrogate for Him (Gen. 31:44-50). It is a stone, similarly, which is declared witness of the covenant of Shechem:

> So Joshua made a covenant for the people on that day; he instituted for them a statute and an ordinance in Shechem. Having written these words in the Book of the Torah of God, Joshua took a great stone and set it up there beneath the terebinth which is in the Lord's sanctuary. Then Joshua said to all the people, "This stone hereby becomes a witness against us, for it has heard all the sayings of the Lord which he has spoken with us; it is thus potentially a witness against you, lest you deal falsely with your God" (Joshua 24:26-27).

The Reubenites and the Gadites declare to their fellow-Israelites that they built the altar at the Jordan

> "... not for burnt offering nor for sacrifice, but to be a witness between us and you and our generations after us ... so that your children not say to ours on some future day, 'You have no portion in the Lord'" ... And the Reubenites and the Gadites had this proclamation made respecting the altar: "It is a witness between us that the Lord is God" (Joshua 22:26-34).

In the following passage, strikingly, we not only have natural phenomena—"the heavens and the earth"—in the office of a living witness, but the written words of a book:

> When Moses had finished writing down in a book the words of this Torah to their very end, he commanded the Levites, as follows: "Take this Book of the Torah, and put it alongside the Ark of the Covenant of the Lord, your God, and it shall be there for a witness against you. For I know your rebellion and your stiff neck: if, while I have been still alive with you, to this day you have been showing rebellion against the Lord, then how much the more after my death? Assemble to me all the elders of your tribes and your officers, that I may speak into their ears all these words, and take the heavens and the earth as witness against them. For I know that after my death you will behave most corruptly and turn aside from the way which I have enjoined upon you; and disaster must light upon you in future days because you will do what is evil in the eyes of the Lord, angering him with the work of your hands" (Deut. 31:24-29).

The written Book of the Torah here is regarded as "witness" to the details of the obedience Israel had agreed to give to the Lord—as witness, that is, to its own content and substance. Moses' reading of this content into the ears of the elders and officers (a required feature, as mentioned above, when divine words depend for fulfillment upon human volition)—the fact, namely, that he had so uttered this content—is to have for its "witness" the entire cosmos, mentioned here in the familiar hendiadys of "heaven and earth." Indeed, apostrophizations of cosmic phenomena in the Hebrew Scriptures, such as

Hear, O heavens, and give ear, O earth  (Isa. 1:2),

are always a summoning of these *ad hoc* "representatives" of their Maker to attest the fact that there has been an utterance, that the words of this utterance are abroad in the world.

The Song of Moses (Deut. 32), which opens with just such an apostraphization—

> "Give ear, O heavens, and I will speak,
> and may the earth hear the sayings of my mouth" (32:1)

—is an excellent example of a written composition expected to function as a living witness. Respecting this Song, Moses and Joshua are enjoined as follows:

> "Now therefore write this Song down, and teach it to the Israelites; put it in their mouths, so that this Song may be a witness for me against the Israelites. For I will bring them into a land flowing with milk and honey, as to which I gave my oath to their fathers, and they shall eat, be filled, and grow fat. But should they run to other gods and serve them, and despise me and break my covenant, then, when many ills and troubles light upon them, this Song will testify before them as a witness; for it will not drop forgotten out of the mouths of their progeny. For I know their inclination, what they are likely to do this very day, even before I bring them into the land as to which I gave my oath." So Moses wrote down this Song on that same day, and taught it to the Israelites (Deut. 31:19-22).

A future, covenant-violating Israel would thus be confronted by a Song, recorded and preserved in writing, which would "testify before them as a witness" that the ills consequently brought upon them were only what they amply deserved and ought to have expected. Here, then, we have a main purpose, as conceived in ancient Israel, of the writing down of productions of literary art: to preserve them and to enable them to present their "testimony" to concerned persons in the future, to make it possible for such persons to understand the significance of the "ills and troubles" by which they might find themselves assailed. A written literary composition, a "witness" to past undertakings—a "witness" also attested by the structure of the cosmos—is available to prove that those past undertakings have been violated by those responsible for carrying them out, in consequence of which the latter are paying the penalties to which they had made themselves liable. This literary production, this written Song, by attesting the past renders the present explicable, hence controllable. That our passage takes for granted the comparing, by concerned readers in the present, of their own life-circumstances with the sanctions of a life-style attested by a written literary text to have been assumed by their predecessors in the historic past, and handed down to them as the *sine qua non* of their continuing group-identity, is richly suggestive of the manner in which literature—especially sacred literature—was thought of as functioning in ancient Israel.

The notion of a written text as constituting a "future witness" is given clear expression in this prophetic instruction:

"Come and write it now on a tablet of theirs,
and inscribe it upon a book,
that it may constitute, at a later day,
a witness forever" (Isa. 30:8).

The written prophecy will not only serve as a witness for the Lord vis-à-vis the Israelites against whom it was originally uttered, but after fulfillment will serve eternally as an attestation of the fact that the Lord so acted. The conception is also plainly in evidence in these lines:

Let this be written down for a subsequent generation,
and people yet to be formed will praise the Lord (Ps. 102:19[18]).

We may certainly see the influence of this notion about writing in the terms "tables of the testimony" (Exod. 31:18, and often), "(God's) testimonies" (e.g., I Kings 2:3), and "attestation" (Isa. 8:16). And the assumption that to write words down may constitute them a "future witness" is further implicit in the many instances when a book or document is appealed to, or cited as evidence; e.g.:

"Is not that written in The Book of the Upright?" (Joshua 10:13; cf. II Sam. 1:18);

... are they not written in The Book of Annals of the Kings of Judah/Israel? (I Kings 14:29/15:31, and often);

... as written in the Book of Moses' Torah ... (Joshua 8:31).

In fine, as the foregoing examples and illustrations suggest, and as will be seen even more clearly farther on in this essay, the assumption that the written word can attest, testify, constitute a "witness," has had consequences of major importance in the literary art of ancient Israel.

### 6. Some Possible Misconceptions of the Argument of this Book

We are now at the end of our exposition of the key assumptions and beliefs that comprise ancient Israel's postulation of literature, and about to commence our exhibition of the impact of that postulation upon the problematic literary phenomena of the Hebrew Bible. This, then, is perhaps the most appropriate juncture at which to forewarn the reader (as I think he/she should be forewarned) against some possible misconceptions of the argument and findings of this book.

First the reader should be aware that the observation of ancient Israel's perception of the nature, properties and powers of words, set forth above, is not the original discovery of the author of this essay. On the contrary, the fact that the words were thought by the writers and editors who produced the Hebrew Scriptures to be instrumentalities of other functions than those involved in communication and expression has been very widely observed and repeatedly demonstrated.[11] The presentation of the matter in this essay, however, differs from its predecessors' in two important respects. It seeks, in the first place, to exhibit and expound the basis in the Hebrew language itself, as viewed by the ancient Israelite writers and editors, of their supposition that words were possessed not only of communicative, but of extra-communicative properties and powers. In the second place, it demonstrates—and this is the task to which the ensuing chapters of this essay are devoted—that ancient Israel's cultural perception of words is definitive of the literary art of the Hebrew Scriptures. The widely recognized ancient Israelite beliefs about the extra-communicative powers of words, while some scholars have seen in them support for their views of Old Testament theology, have never hitherto been brought to bear on the problems presented by the Hebrew Scriptures *as literature.*[12]

---

[11] See J. L. Lindblom, *Prophecy in Ancient Israel* (Oxford, 1962), 51f., 114f., 172, 203; G. von Rad, *Old Testament Theology* II (Edinburgh, 1965), 80f.; and the abundant previous literature cited in these two works.

[12] Except, of course, in the two papers cited in note 2, above. Having read the first of those papers, the late W. F. Albright wrote me about it, as follows: "It is curious that a point like this, which many of us know theoretically, should never have been stressed, as far as I know. I certainly have not made the point anywhere in my own writings, but I hope to in the future, with due reference to your own fine essay." Cf. his *Yahweh and the Gods of Canaan* (London, 1968), 188-189.

No reader, secondly, should imagine that this essay asserts, claims or suggests *uniqueness* for the literature of the Hebrew Bible on any grounds whatever, including those involved in ancient Israel's cultural perception of literature as herein presented. *Distinctiveness, differentness* in many respects from the beliefs and assumptions involved in our *modern western* cultural postulation of literature—yes. Such differentness is frequently pointed out because the contrast enables us more clearly to see, and more easily to grasp, the ancient Israelite percept or concept under discussion. But the differentness or distinctiveness of ancient Israel's beliefs about literature from those prevalent in modern western societies, which is asserted in this essay, must not be misconstrued into a claim that the Hebrew Bible, as literature, is unique, without parallel in the literature of any literate culture anywhere in the ancient or modern world. On the contrary, the ancient Israelite assumptions—particularly the beliefs about words and their connection with the "realities" that in modern western cultures words are held to symbolize or represent—are known to be widely shared with many other cultures. They have been detected in the orally transmitted texts of modern preliterate societies;[13] they are even vestigially present in our modern western cultures, insofar as the texts of spells, charms, incantations, and the like, continue to be functional amongst us.[14] Nor can there be any doubt that the literatures of ancient Egypt and of the ancient Near East, in so many detailed respects so obviously like and related to the literature of the Hebrew Bible, embody and reflect much the same set of basic beliefs and conceptions as those shown in this

---

[13] See, e.g., B. Malinowski, *Argonauts of the Western Pacific* (London, 1932), 427; E. Cassirer, *Language and Myth* (New York, 1946), 44f.; Toshihiko Izutsu, *Language and Magic* (Tokyo, Keio Institute of Philological Studies, 1965), *passim*.

[14] R. C. Elliott, *The Power of Satire: Magic, Ritual, Art* (Princeton, 1960), 15, while recognizing a relationship between magic and satire, distinguishes "between ... magical satire and the more familiar magical spells known the world over. The magical spell has a set, invariable form; its efficacy depends on getting the spell 'right', that is, uttering it exactly according to the established formula. Magical satire, on the other hand, is usually extemporaneous and each satirical utterance unique."

essay to be operative in the literature of ancient Israel.[15]
While no such detailed tracing-out of the relationship between
literary texts and their underlying assumptions as presented
here in regard to ancient Israel has yet been done in the specific
instances of the other ancient Near Eastern cultures, it is virtually certain that this can—I believe ultimately will—be done.[16]

The last of the several possible misconceptions of the thesis
and findings of this essay against which the reader should be
warned is the notion that the Old Testament is not really "literature" at all, and cannot, or ought not, be read and studied as
such. This is a misconception that I have heard voiced repeatedly by students throughout a long career of discussing the
books of the Old Testament. Not only so, but it is a misconception shared by many thoughtful western literary scholars and
critics, among them such eminent writers as T. S. Eliot and C.
S. Lewis. The former, denouncing "the men of letters ... who
talk of the Bible ... as 'literature'," contrasts the Bible's religious
importance with its small value as literature: "The Bible," he
says, "has had a *literary* influence upon English literature *not*
because it has been considered as literature, but because it has
been considered as the report of the Word of God."[17] C. S.
Lewis, similarly contrasting the literary and "the religious
claims of the Bible," has written: "It is ... not merely a sacred
book, but a book so remorselessly and continuously sacred that
it does not invite, it excludes or repels, the merely aesthetic
approach. You can read it as literature only by a *tour de force*."[18]

---

[15] See the discussion by P. Heimisch, *Das "Wort" im Alten Testament und in alten Orient* (Münster, 1923); L. Dürr, *Die Wertung des göttlichen Wortes im Alten Testament und in antiken Orient* (Leipzig, 1938); and H. Masing, *The Word of Yaweh* (Tartu, 1936), to mention only these.

[16] In the case of ancient Mesopotamian religious literature, note, for example, T. Jacobsen, *The Treasures of Darkness: A History of Mesopotamian Religion* (New Haven, 1976), 15: "Poetry was another means of invoking the presence of the powers, for word pictures, too, created the correspond-ing reality.... The creative power of the word underlies all Mesopotamian religious literature."

[17] T. S. Eliot, "Religion and Literature," in *Essays Ancient and Modern* (New York, 1936), 95-96.

[18] C. S. Lewis, *The Literary Impact of the Authorized Version* (Philadelphia, 1967), 32-33.

In the culture of ancient Israel, it must be pointed out, religion was not as distinctively separate from other aspects of life as the statements of these literary scholars suggest. The producers of the Hebrew Scriptures could neither have conceived the idea of a book of religion that was not a work of literature, nor could they have thought that any literary creation—no matter how "empty" or "foolish" (as they might say, instead of "secular" or "profane")—was totally devoid of implications for religion. More to the present point, Eliot's and Lewis' doubt that the Bible is literature is not merely contradicted by our experience-based intuition that it is indeed literature, though of a very "strange" sort. Their doubt is unjustified by virtue of the error of its implied assertion, namely, that "literature" can only be, must exclusively be, what is so considered by our western cultural tradition. That the Hebrew Bible *is* literature, though of a different sort from that otherwise typical of western culture, need therefore not be doubted. If the Hebrew Scriptures are not understood as their creators in *their* culture understood literature to be and to function, we shall not really be able to understand those Scriptures at all.

# CHAPTER THREE

## SOME "ANOMALOUS" LITERARY AND RHETORICAL CONSEQUENCES OF ANCIENT ISRAEL'S PERCEPTION OF LITERATURE

As remarked above, the culturally distinctive ancient Israelite assumptions about the nature and power of words, and about the composition and functioning of texts are responsible for much that strikes us as bizarre or anomalous in ancient Israel's literature. A number of instances of such phenomena will now be pointed out: some literary and rhetorical examples in the present chapter, and, in the next, some of the passages that exhibit the more specifically textual consequences of the underlying conception of "holy words." Obviously licit and understandable in terms of ancient Israel's perception of literature, these passages will be seen to turn upon data quite outside the limits of what western readers are conditioned to regard as normal and permissible. Really to understand them demands of us the effort to comprehend and appreciate the assumptions that comprise ancient Israel's postulation of literature, and to read them in terms of those assumptions.[19]

### 1. Words as Future Historical "Realities"

Jeremiah's autobiographical account of how the Lord commissioned him as prophet, and of what, as such, he

---

[19] Readers will find it instructive to compare the treatment here of the "strange" literary phenomena of these passages with that of other commentators (e.g., the notes in H. G. May and B. M. Metzger, eds., *The Oxford Annotated Bible ... : Revised Standard Version* [New York, 1973], or those in S. Sandmel, ed., *The New English Bible ... : Oxford Study Edition* [New York, 1976]). That these seemingly anomalous phenomena are "saved" in the light of ancient Israel's postulation of literature, while remaining inexplicable or obscure in the perspective of modern western literary conventions, is additional proof of the validity of the argument of this book.

would be charged to accomplish, while scarcely comprehensible if taken seriously in terms of modern western literary and rhetorical conventions, are completely explicable and "natural" if read in the light of ancient Israel's assumptions as to the nature and powers of words. "The word of the Lord," Jeremiah says, "came to me, saying"

> "'Before forming you in the womb, I knew you, and before you went forth from the uterus, I consecrated you:
>
> I have made you a Nations'-Prophet.'
>
> "At this I said: 'Ah, Lord God, I am obviously untrained in speaking, for I am just a boy.'
>
> But the Lord said to me:
>
> 'Do not say "I am just a boy";
> for on whatsoever mission I send you, you shall go, and whatsoever I command you, you shall speak.
>
> Do not be afraid of them,
> for I shall be with you to preserve you,'
>     declared the Lord.
>
> "Then the Lord extended his hand and brought it over my mouth; and the Lord said to me:
>
> 'I hereby set my words in your mouth. See, I have commissioned you this day over the nations
>
> and over the kingdoms,
>         to pull up and to pull down,
>         and to destroy and to overthrow,
>         and to build up and to plant.'"      (Jer. 1:4-10)

Note the—to us—astonishing presumptions of this passage: Jeremiah, a mere boy, is divinely commissioned to effect the overthrow and destruction of certain powerful, well-armed nations and kingdoms, and to bring about the upbuilding and firm establishment of other such political aggregates. How is he to do this? Not, so far as anything in this or any other passage suggests, by coming himself into command of armed forces capable of accomplishing such ends and purposes. He is just *to speak*—and the speaking is presumed to be potentially dangerous to his own life—the words which the Lord would command him to utter. These words of the Lord, sent *via* Jeremiah into the world, were plainly regarded as the means whereby the prophet would carry out the Lord's commission; the words were to compass—were to constitute—the destruction of some political entities, and the upbuilding of others. The words are not here thought of as the means whereby the prophet would induce others—the necessary armed forces, for example—to effect the stated ends. The words are rather thought of as themselves the very historical realities, the *future* overthrowings and upbuildings of principalities and powers which—again, to us—as symbols of communication they express. The words which Jeremiah, as "Nations'-Prophet," was to utter were thought of as constitutive of realities in the same way as, to the writer of Gen. 1:3, light was constituted and instituted by God's words, "Let light come to be."

Not less impervious to understanding without recourse to ancient Israelite beliefs regarding words and word-groupings is the divine directive given the prophet Isaiah in the course of the latter's famous Temple vision:

> When I heard the voice of the Lord saying,
>     "Whom shall I send?
>     And who will go for us?"
> I said, "Here am I: send me."
> Thereupon he said, "Go and say to this people:
>     'Hear, indeed, and do not understand;
>     See, indeed, and do not come to know,'
>     Stupefy the mind of this people,
>     Dull its ears,
>     Lest, seeing with its eyes,
>         hearing with its ears,
>         and understanding with its mind,
>     It come to repent,
> And so heal itself" (Isa. 6:8-10).

How, on that conception of Israel's prophets which views them as "preachers," and their words as "sermons" and "exhortations," are we to understand the commission that God is here stated to have enjoined upon Isaiah? Instead of bringing the people to understanding, repentance and healing, he is bidden to prevent them from achieving understanding, repentance and healing. As shown by the next following verse (6:11),

> Then I said, "How long, O Lord?" and he said,
>     "Until cities are too ruined to have inhabitant,
>     And houses to have people;
>     And the soil becomes a desolate waste-land,"

the divine intention to visit destruction upon the people as an organized polity had now been made irrevocable. The meaning of God's commission to the prophet was that he was to bring about the condition in the people which would preclude any possibility of revocation of the now determined and decreed destruction. How was Isaiah to accomplish this mission? According to our passage, he was to speak the words "Hear, indeed," etc. "to this people"—not, however, to persuade them to hear, see and understand (as, if the words were thought of as purely communicative, we should naturally suppose), but rather to produce in them the contrary effect: to prevent them from hearing, seeing, understanding. Since the prevention here indicated was to be accomplished through the speaking of these particular words, persuasiveness—communication designed to convince—clearly does not exhaust the significance of the words. A hearing or sighted person might be persuaded that what he is hearing or seeing is something other than what he actually hears or sees, but physical prevention of others from hearing or seeing is not an effect that, by our cultural assumptions, can be accomplished by a speaker's addressing words to others, however persuasive those words might be.

Here, then, the reality-to-be—the precluding of the revocation of the divinely decreed destruction of the people as an organized polity—was to be accomplished, indeed was constituted, just by the utterance—the speaking out loud "to this people"—of the words Isaiah was bidden by the Lord to utter. Both this passage and that of Jeremiah's commissioning as prophet, cited above, are thus explicable only in terms of the assumption, alien to our culture but taken for granted in that of ancient Israel, that words and texts could be the very pith and substance, the very actuality, of future history and historical reality.

## 2. Words Directed to Unwitting or Insentient Addresses

A rhetorical technique found often in the Hebrew Scriptures—one that by our western standards seems too self-
contradictory and anomalous to be literally admissible—is the
speech addressed to an audience that cannot possibly hear, read,
or understand what is spoken. Jeremiah, for example, is bidden,

> "Go and proclaim these words toward the north, and say:
> 'Return, O apostate Israel, declares the Lord ...'" (Jer. 3:12).

At this juncture, as we know from the context of the passage,
Jeremiah is in Judea, and the apostate Israelites, the designated audience of the speech, are far away, in the territories
of the North and East whither the Assyrians exiled them. The
directive given the prophet, therefore, meant that he was so
to orient himself while speaking out the words of the divine
declaration that the words might issue forth in the direction
of the physical locale of the Israelites who were to receive the
impact, and enact the content, of those words. The words are
here thought of as the future reality of Israel's repentance
("return"), sent into the quarter of the world where Israel
then was located.

Ezekiel is in Babylonia, far removed from Pharaoh and
Egypt, when, the prophet writes,

> ... the word of the Lord came to me: "Son of man, set your
> face against Pharaoh king of Egypt, and prophesy against
> him and against all Egypt. Speak, and say,
>
>> 'Thus said the Lord God:
>> Behold, I am against you,
>> Pharaoh, king of Egypt,
>> the great dragon that lies sprawled in the midst of
>>       his streams,'" etc. [29:1-3].

By means of this speech—which, though addressed to
Pharaoh in the second person singular, that monarch could
neither hear nor be aware of—the future destruction and
desolation of Egypt was thought to be now ushered into the
world and awaiting fulfillment.

The prophet Isaiah and Hezekiah king of Judah are in
Jerusalem, and Sennacherib king of Assyria is some distance
away, "warring against Libnah," when, we are told, Isaiah

sends this message to Hezekiah:

> "Thus says the Lord, the God of Israel: 'Because you
> prayed to me regarding Sennacherib king of Assyria, this
> is the word which the Lord has pronounced against him:
>
>> 'She despises you,
>> She scorns you
>>         —the virgin daughter of Zion;
>> she wags her head behind you
>>         —the daughter of Jerusalem.'" etc.
>>                 [Isa. 37:21f.= II Kings 19:20f.].

The speech promises—indeed constitutes the word-form
of—the salvation of Hezekiah, Jerusalem and the Judean
kingdom from destruction at the hands of Sennacherib, the
Assyrian king. The taunt-prophecy is addressed to Sennacherib in the second person singular, though of course he could
not hear it, nor is there any statement to the effect that it was
written and sent to him for perusal. From the point of view
of a modern western reader, the narrative-context of this
taunt-prophecy only emphasizes the strangeness of the fact
that it was neither heard nor read by Sennacherib, for the
context, as it happens, makes it explicitly clear that the
address could easily have been written down and sent to the
Assyrian king, or to Rab-shakeh, his envoy. It was a letter
sent by Rab-shakeh to Hezekiah, we are told, that caused the
Judean king to pray to the Lord for salvation from the hand
of the Assyrian; stranger still, we note that the text of the
taunt in which Sennacherib is directly addressed was *sent* by
Isaiah—but to Hezekiah, not to Sennacherib (Isa. 37:21 = II Kings
19:20).

Since the divine words introduced into the world at the
mouth of a prophet were in ancient Israel held to constitute
a creation (or a destruction) of some kind, it is quite in keeping to read of speeches addressed to "audiences" that consist
not of sentient human beings, but of physical and geographical phenomena. Ezekiel, for example, is in Babylonia at the
moment he is given this divine directive:

> "Son of man, set your face in the direction of Teman, distill
> speech to the South, and prophesy to the forest of the open
> country in the Negeb. Say to the forest of the Negeb: 'Hear

the word of the Lord! Thus says the Lord God: Behold, I
am about to set a fire in you, and it will consume every
green tree in you and every dry tree. No flame of the fire
shall be put out, but all faces from the Negeb northward
shall be scorched by it.' And all flesh shall see that it is I,
the Lord, who have set it afire; it will not be put out"
(Ezek. 21:1-4[20:45-48]).

The unquenchable forest fire adumbrated in this passage was
to be a "sign" that the impending destruction of the Judean
polity, an event that would ultimately affect the whole of
mankind, was God's doing. That fiery "sign" was ushered
into incipient reality through the speech to the forest—a
speech pronounced by a man hundreds of miles away who,
using the second person singular of direct address, thus
apostrophized his insentient "audience." Ezekiel's reaction
to this directive is indicative of his awareness that the speech
was designed to create a physical reality, and was not the
verbal "likeness" composed by himself that some of his
contemporaries might take it to be: "Then I said: Alas, O my
Lord God! They are saying of me, 'Is he not a propounder of
parables?'" (21:5 [20:49]). Other such insentient "audiences"
are comprised of mountains (Ezek. 6:2f., 36:1f.), human
bones and breath (Ezek. 37:4-10), and the altar at Beth-el (I
Kings 13:2), to mention only these.

The "bizarre" convention of ancient Israelite rhetoric
exemplified in this section is the *sine qua non* of understanding the many prophecies addressed to foreign nations and
kings in the several prophetic books; Isa. 13-23, Jer. 46-51 and
Ezek. 25-32 are made up of such materials. In the case of none
of these prophecies are we given to understand that the
person or persons addressed ever heard or read it. Such
utterances are in fact inexplicable on our modern western
assumption that a prophecy must always and only have been
a message, a communication of some kind, that was necessarily addressed to an audience capable of hearing or reading it. But as perceived in ancient Israel—as the reality
constituted and named by its words—a prophet's speech did
not necessarily require an audience at all.

### 3. Wishes or Hopes Stated as Accomplished Actualities

Very odd from the standpoint of our western literary conventions is the ancient Israelite rhetorical device wherein a speaker or writer states as an accomplished actuality an effect or event that he would like to see brought about, but that in fact has not come to pass, and indeed may never happen. Jonah's prayer—2:2(1) so categorizes his speech from the belly of the great fish assigned by the Lord to swallow him—is a prime example of this device. His prayer consists of an account of how, when he was in a life-threatening strait which is described as if it were now past and done with, he called upon the Lord, and the Lord answered him, and saved his life:

> "I called, out of a strait of mine, to the Lord,
> and he answered me;
> from the belly of Sheol did I cry out,
> and thou didst hear my voice ...
> and thou didst bring my life up from the Pit,
> O Lord, my God!" (2:3[2], 7[6]).

Especially to be noted in this psalm is Jonah's vagueness as to the exact nature of the "previous" deathly peril from which he says the Lord rescued him. As described by him, it was either one in which he was threatened by drowning (2:4-6[3-5]), or else one in which he was in danger of being swallowed up forever in the bowels of the earth (2:7[6]). This vagueness is not merely a nice touch: Jonah, in the belly of the fish, could not know just how his life would end, if end it must. It is necessarily a corollary of, and so a clue to, the rhetorical device which is here being employed. The plight from which Jonah describes himself as already rescued is none other than the very plight from which, by means of this rhetorical device, he is in course of petitioning the Lord now to rescue him; hence the imprecision as to the kind of death confronted.

Expressed as a psalm of thanksgiving for a rescue declared already accomplished, Jonah's prayer for deliverance consists of the sort of laudation of the Lord that he would pronounce if in fact he should be delivered out of his present strait. It is a hymn of thanks-in-advance for the salvific act hoped for and thus rhetorically petitioned—an expression which, God willing, would become the human witness-text of the divine deliverance that might thus be triggered into actualization. And that God was so willing in this instance is declared by 2:11(10): "Then the Lord gave the order to the fish, and it disgorged Jonah onto the dry land."

Psalm 85 exhibits a somewhat different form of our "anomalous" rhetorical device. The opening verses consist of an account of several apparently past acts of the Lord's grace:

> Thou hast shown favor, O Lord, to thy land,
> Thou hast restored the captivity of Jacob.
> Thou hast forgiven the iniquity of thy people,
> Thou hast covered away all their sin. *Selah.*
> Thou hast withdrawn all thy rage,
> Thou hast turned back from all thy burning wrath (2-4[1-3]).

Immediately following, however, we have a prayer for the enactment of these same events, a group of verses in which the salvific acts are treated not as past and accomplished, but as future and hoped for:

> Restore us, O God of our salvation,
> And annul thy vexation with us!
> Wilt thou be angry with us forever,
> Protract thy wrath for generations?
> Is it not thou that art to restore us to life,
> Thy people those that are to rejoice in thee?
> Show us, O Lord, thy gracious love,
> And grant us thy salvation (5-8[4-7]).

In this form of the rhetorical device, accordingly, the actual prayer makes explicit, and so buttresses and reinforces, the implicit prayer of the statement of the Lord's "past acts" of grace. The prayer is a plea that the Lord make actualities of the word-forms of the acts attributed to Him in the opening verses as already His accomplishments.

Modern commentators and translators, unaware of the Psalmist's use of a rhetorical gambit quite alien to our western literary tradition, have not unnaturally experienced difficulty in treating Psalm 85's seemingly bizarre collocation of a statement of already accomplished "facts" with a petition for future enactment of those same facts. In two instances, which

we may briefly notice here, the translators' attempts to exorcise
the awkwardness have caused them to make unjustified
additions to the text of the psalm. The Revised Standard
Version, treating the petitionary verses (5-8[4-7]) as a prayer
for a *repetition* of the salvific acts listed as "past" in the opening verses(2-4[1-3]), inserts the word "again" in verse 5[4]:
"Restore us *again*, O God of our salvation." But there is no
"again" in the Hebrew original. In the widely used Well-
hausen-Furness version of the Psalter,[20] on the other hand,
the prayer is construed as having preceded, and resulted in,
the effects narrated in the opening verses; contemplated here
are not *two* separate series of salvific acts, as in the RSV, but
merely one. This view of the connection between the state-
ment-of-facts and the prayer has, however, constrained these
scholars to intrude between verses 4(3) and 5(4) an entire
sentence—"In the bygone days of distress, we said"—no
syllable of which represents anything in the underlying
Hebrew text. Once our ancient Israelite rhetorical technique
is understood, of course, the "anomalousness" of the collocation is dissipated, and "explanatory" additions to the text
are seen to be unnecessary.

Psalm 126 affords another example of the rhetorical
usage in which the statement of a seemingly past event is
followed (and contradicted) by the prayer for its enactment
(126:4). The device is more commonly exemplified, however,
in its form as implicit prayer, without additional words of
explicit prayer. It is most generally found in contexts which
leave the reader under no misapprehension as to the reality
of the assertedly past "facts," contexts which make it clear
that those "facts" are being viewed by the author(s) from a
time-perspective imaginatively projected as beyond that in
which they were supposedly accomplished. Very often,
accordingly, we find the usage in the context of one or
another phase of the "end of days" or of the post-eschaton
dispensation confidently expected according to scriptural
prophecy. Thus, in Psalm 98, verses 2-3 treat God's eschatological victory as won, and now past; in Psalm 99, the Lord,

---

[20] J. Wellhausen and H. H. Furness, *The Book of Psalms: A New English Translation* (New York, 1898), 89-90, 199.

conceived as now entered upon His ultimate sovereignty and enthroned upon the cherubim in Zion, is declared to have already executed justice and righteousness through Jacob; and in Psalm 47, verse 9(8) states that God, now King over the nations, has seated Himself upon His holy throne.

This rhetorical device, ambiguous and puzzling though it may seem to modern translators and readers of the Hebrew Bible, is the quite natural literary consequence of the ancient Israelite assumption that words are concentrated essences of the things, acts and events they name and characterize. Since all created realities are initially words, the words uttered by human beings may, God willing, come to full scope as those realities. Hence, to say that something one hopes for has already occurred, even though this may not be the case, is to introduce the necessary initial phase of that occurrence into the world, and, in effect, to invite God to bring it fully to pass. Whether expressing joy or sorrow, triumph or lamentation, the device always implies a petition to God that its allegation of "fact" come to be the full reality it asserts as already in the world.

### 4. The "Booking" of Future "Realities"

If Exodus 17:14 seems "strange" and "obscure" to a modern reader, this is because the statements of the verse turn upon several points of difference between ancient Israel's culturally received perception of the two primary literary activities—the writing and reading of a text—and that of our modern western societies. Following the account of how Israel, led by Joshua, defeated the Amalekites in Rephidim (Exodus 17:8-13), we read the following:

> And the Lord said to Moses: "Write this, a remembrance-record, in the book, and put it in Joshua's ears: that I will utterly blot out the remembrance of Amalek from under the heavens" (17:14).

Now we know from other passages (e.g., Josh. 1:8 and 8:32) that Joshua was able to read. To modern readers, accordingly, it seems quite strange that Moses, instead of being instructed by the Lord to show Joshua the written statement in the book, and to let him read it for himself, is instructed to "put it in Joshua's ears," that is, to read it aloud to Joshua, so that the latter should hear it. Why, if Joshua could read the statement, should Moses have had to read it out loud to him? Our sense of "strangeness" here, we realize, proceeds from our modern western assumption that the purport of the Lord's instruction to Moses was merely that he *communicate* to Joshua the content of the written "remembrance-record," namely, the Lord's promise to exterminate the Amalekites. There is no "strangeness," of course, once we glimpse the less restricted ancient Israelite assumptions implicit in the Lord's instructions to Moses. If Moses was required not merely to write and show the "remembrance-record" to a literate Joshua, but to read it out loud in the latter's hearing, this plainly was because, as the ancient Israelites viewed the matter, an act of reading out such a text to another person was presumed to be efficacious of a purpose that transcended the communicating of the content of that text. What that purpose was has already been mentioned above: a text composed of divine words, if deliberately uttered aloud in the physical hearing of whatever person or persons upon whose volition the fulfillment of the words might wholly or partly depend, was thought to constitute an initial act of such fulfillment on the part of the divine, as well as a commitment on the part of the human beings involved that they might breach only at peril of their condign punishment. The words creative of that fulfillment, once so pronounced aloud, were now in the world, and, when heard, would enter the souls of the hearers, those who were to play a part in fully actualizing them. Joshua here personifies Israel's future leadership, those upon whom the fulfillment of the Lord's threat against the Amalekites would in part depend. The same assumption, we note, also underlies the narrative of the covenanting on Mount Sinai:

> Now when Moses had written down all the words of the Lord.... he took the book of the covenant and read it aloud in the people's ears; and they said: "All that the Lord has spoken we will do, that we may obey" (Exodus 24:4-7).

As the Israelites present at Sinai-Horeb personify and represent the Israel of future generations—"And not with you only do I make this covenant ... but with him standing here with us today ... and with him not here with us today" (Deut. 29:13-14)—so Joshua in the passage under discussion personifies and represents the future leadership of Israel.

Quite possibly, the book in which Moses was directed to write the "remembrance-record" was *The Book of the Upright* (Chapter Five, below). Wherever booked, the "remembrance-record" was obviously intended to be read again upon occasions subsequent to its initial reading "in Joshua's ears." Each such reading would attest the fact that the Lord's purpose to destroy Amalek was in the world awaiting complete fulfillment, and would recommit the leadership of Israel to do their part in the accomplishment of that purpose. Each such reading would also be a delicate "reminder" to the Lord that his promise, the word-form of the future historical reality, was on attested record in the "book": it would in effect be a petition, a prayer, addressed to the Lord for the fulfillment of His word. And when, ultimately, the words of the "booked reality" should have come fully to be the case, the words would thereafter constitute a precious additional witness of the Lord's sure uprightness, an earnest that other recorded words of His would similarly be brought to their full scope.[21]

*5. The Reading-out of "Booked Realities" as Means of their Effectuation*

In ancient Israel, the motives, circumstances and impact of an act of reading—the pronouncing aloud of a composed, or a composed-and-written, text—were not necessarily thought to be confined, as in our modern western cultures we generally suppose, to the processes involved in communicating and apprehending written groupings of ordered words. From a modern western point of view, indeed, the cultural assump-

---

[21] The liturgical reading of the Scriptures practiced to this day in synagogues and churches derives, it will be realized, from the much older cultural assumptions and beliefs exemplified in the foregoing section. Cf. too, the account of the reading of the Torah by Ezra in the sight and hearing of the people gathered in "the square before the Water Gate" (Neh. 8:1-8).

tions about reading reflected in the following passage could
scarcely be more alien:

> The word which Jeremiah the prophet enjoined upon
> Seraiah, son of Neriah son of Mahseiah, when Seraiah, be-
> ing quarter-master, went with Zedekiah king of Judah to
> Babylon in the fourth year of his reign; now Jeremiah had
> written the whole of the disaster which was to come upon
> Babylon into a single book—all these words that are writ-
> ten respecting Babylon. And Jeremiah said to Seraiah:
> "When, coming to Babylon, you see it, read out all these
> words, and then say: 'O Lord, it was *thou* who didst speak
> towards this place so as to destroy it, so that it harbor no
> inhabitant, neither man nor cattle, but be a desolation for-
> ever.' And when you have finished the reading-out of this
> book, you shall tie a stone to it, hurl it into the midst of the
> Euphrates, and say: 'Thus shall Babylon sink; nor shall she
> rise again, because of the disaster which I am bringing
> upon her'" (Jer. 51:59-64).

The words of the prophetic doom upon Babylon which
Jeremiah had written "into a single book," (i.e., a scroll) and
given to the quartermaster, Seraiah, for use as directed, are
undoubtedly those before us in chapters 50-51 of our Book
of Jeremiah. The phrase in our passage, "all these words that
are written respecting Babylon," is plainly a reference to
these two chapters; and verses in both chapters (50:39-40 and
51:37, 43) are specifically referred to in the appeal to the Lord
that Seraiah was to utter (v. 62). The "book" given to Seraiah
consisted, accordingly, of a copy of the Lord's "word ...
concerning Babylon" which he had "spoken through the
prophet Jeremiah" (Jer. 50:1). Since the "book" was a copy,
we note that Jeremiah had already written that divine
"word" (51:60; cf. 36:2); and even before that, in performance
of his prophetic office, as pointed out above (cf. Jer. 1:4-10),
he had already uttered it. This utterance—so he and other
Israelites believed—had created the reality-to-be of Babylon's disaster, and had introduced it into the world, where
it awaited fulfillment at such time as the Lord might will. In
fine, the production-sequence and directed reading-out of
the text given Seraiah, according to our passage, consisted of
(1) the Lord's creation, through the word given Jeremiah to
utter, of the doom upon Babylon; (2) the recording of this

prophecy along with other prophecies now in the Book of Jeremiah (36:2); (3) Jeremiah's copying of the recorded prophecy against Babylon "into a single book," which he turned over to Seraiah; and (4) Seraiah's reading-out of the words of the book, as instructed. Clearly, the reading-out of the words is thought of as made possible by, but not necessarily as constituting the main purpose of, their having been uttered and then written down.

Jeremiah's instructions to Seraiah were also four-fold. Seraiah was (a) to read out the book within sight of Babylon; (b) to conclude the reading-out with a prayerful address to the Lord; (c) to execute, by means of the book-scroll, an act of sympathetic magic; and (d) to accompany this ceremonious action with a spoken incantation. These several instructions, we note, are based upon assumptions and beliefs regarding literature which are directly contradictory of, and alien to, western beliefs. Jeremiah's "book," we first observe, contained passages addressed to Babylon, in which, speaking to Babylon, the Lord says "you":

> O you that dwell beside many waters,
> abundant in treasures,
> Your end has come,
> the measured term of your profiteering (Jer. 51:13).

Yet neither at Seraiah's reading-out, nor when Jeremiah first pronounced the words, was any Babylonian on hand to hear the doom thus expressed. Here, then, is yet another example of the ancient Hebrew literary convention, pointed out above, whereby a prophet may speak words—particularly the Lord's words—to an *absent* or to an *unwitting* addressee. As in other instances in which the prophet is told to orient himself so that the divine words are spoken out in the direction of the distant physical locale of whoever or whatever is to receive the impact of those words (e.g., Jer. 3:12 and Ezek. 21:1-4[20:45-48]), so here (in Jer. 51:61) reference is made to the Lord's speaking "towards this place."

A second difference in cultural perception is detectable in Jeremiah's instruction that Seraiah was to read out the words of the "book" when, coming to Babylon, he should see the city. Since the words of the "book" had presumably

already been uttered by Jeremiah himself in Judea, and since,
by the convention just previously noted, such words did not
necessarily require to be uttered in the *hearing* of those to
whom they were directly addressed, some greater efficacy
must have been felt to attach to words of doom or of blessing
if pronounced within the physical *sight* of the intended recipient of the impact of the words. We have already noticed, in
our discussion of Exodus 17:14, the ancient Israelite cultural
distinction respecting the *hearing* of divine words: such hearing was considered essential only if the words involved some
action dependent upon the recipient's volition, for example,
the carrying-out of a divine commandment; but if, as in the
case of a divinely-ordained, unconditional doom, the impact
of the words did not depend upon the recipient's volition,
the latter need not have heard the utterance. The greater efficacy attributed to doom-words spoken within physical sight
of their target is further illustrated by the story of Balak's
invitation to Balaam to *come* to Moab and, from a place where
the people of Israel could be *seen*, to curse them (Num. 22:4
and 23:13). The role that Balak would have assigned to
Balaam vis-à-vis the Israelites, as recounted in Numbers 22-
24, is the analogue of that assigned to Seraiah vis-à-vis Babylon
in our Jeremiah-passage. The importance attached to the *sight-
ing* of the target of doom-words was doubtless based on the
notion of words as concentrates of palpable realities (Chapter One, above), hence capable of being *aimed* and launched
as missiles. This feature of our Jeremiah-passage and of the
Balak-Balaam narratives in Numbers must remain inexplicable without recourse to the ancient Israelite beliefs and
assumptions that are, of course, not operative in modern
western culture.

Seraiah's reading-out of the book's doom upon Babylon
was to be followed by an apostrophization of the Lord: "'O
Lord, it was *thou* who didst speak towards this place so as to
destroy it,'" etc. In the Hebrew, the "thou" is very emphatic;
Seraiah is saying that the words he has read out from the
book are not his own, not those of any human agent, but
those of the Lord God Himself. The significance is that he
who uttered the words that created and brought forth the

heavens and the earth has thus similarly created the destruction of Babylon. Those words, already in the world, but awaiting actualization, have now again been uttered in sight of their target. What man could do to bring about the fulfillment of the words of the Lord has now been done; the rest, the full actualization, is up to Him. The repetition of the words of the Lord, and the following apostrophization thus constitute a tactful petition, a prayer, for that full actualization. Here, then, we have one of the motives for the reading-out of recorded "holy words": insofar as such words are "booked realities" that remain to be fully actualized, each repetition will be a prayer that may trigger such effectuation.

Finally, the act of sympathetic magic and the incantation which were to follow the reading-out and the apostrophization—note that the incantation-statement (v. 63) identifies the actuality of the disaster as the *words* of the disaster—are to be understood as a means of expressing complete faith that the prayer for effectuation would be answered.

------

Enough has now been said to demonstrate the fact that the cultural postulation of literature in ancient Israel differed greatly from that of our own and other western societies. It should be evident from the examples of Biblical texts studied above that we miss the original sense and purport of those texts if we simply assume that the suppositions and expectations in regard to literature were the same in both ancient Israel's culture and in our own modern western culture—if, indeed, we try to approach those texts from the vantage-point of any save their creators' beliefs and notions about literature.

# CHAPTER FOUR

## Textual Consequences of Ancient Israel's Conception of "Holy Words"

The presence of "holy words" in the Hebrew Scriptures—words believed by the ancient Israelites who wrote them down, read them and heard them to compose foci of immense power as well as to be so many concentrates of the world's realities, past, present and future—has entailed a number of important consequences for the structure and parlance of the Scriptures. These consequences, while they are more specifically textual in character than the literary and rhetorical phenomena exhibited above, and while they are more editorial and redactional than compositional in origin, are no less bizarre and anomalous from the point of view of our modern conceptions regarding the presentation of texts. Unless, therefore, we approach these effects in terms of the ancient Israelite assumptions and conceptions which figure in them and of which they are the products, we may easily find ourselves at a loss to comprehend the passages in which they occur.

As already suggested, two particularly important kinds of literary anomaly have been engendered by editorial care in the handling of "holy words." One kind, especially evident in the books of literary prophecy, is comprised of methods and devices employed in the ordering and sequence of textual materials. The other consists of the conflation—the fusing of variant readings into a single composite reading—produced as a result of editorial efforts to deal with problems of textual variation. Some representative examples of the many instances in the Hebrew Scriptures of each kind of such phenomena will be presented in this chapter. Additionally, since the effects that we shall be studying are editorial or redactional in origin—are the work, that is to say, of the ancient Israelite compilers, editors and redactors, unknown to us by name, who brought together and arranged the texts before us in the Scriptures—we will first notice several of the many indications in the Scriptures of such persons' actuality and presence.

*1. The Editorial or Redactional "Hand" as Manifested in the Scriptures*

The editors and redactors who produced the effects to be studied in this chapter should not be confused with the Massoretes, the scholars who developed the means of safe-guarding the letter-for-letter transmission of the consonantal Hebrew text, and who ultimately affixed its vowel-signs and accents. The Massoretes began their work after the final determination of the fixed authoritative corpus of the Hebrew Scriptures, after, that is to say, the Second Revolt against Rome of 132-135 C.E.; even before this, as we now know from study of ancient biblical manuscripts recently recovered from caves and grottoes in the Judean Wilderness, the text which became that of the Massoretes was being transmitted with scrupulous care and fidelity. But the period of time in which the editors and redactors we are here concerned with were active is that centuries-long epoch during which each book of the Hebrew Bible first achieved its present textual disposition and format—the long period which goes back to at least the downfall of the Judean State in 587 B.C.E. and comes down to approximately the first century C.E.

Judging by the Qumran-cave manuscript-discoveries, all the books of our Hebrew Scriptures except possibly the Book of Esther were in existence by approximately 150 B.C.E.[22] In several passages of at least two non-biblical Qumran scroll-texts there is even a designation, "Book of Meditation" or "Book of Study" (*Sēpher Hehāghō* or *Sēpher Haheghe*), for the collectivity of the books that came later to be called "the Holy Scriptures" and "the Bible." In this expression we have the earliest designation thus far known for Pentateuch *plus*

---

[22] F. M. Cross, Jr., *The Ancient Library of Qumran and Modern Biblical Stud-ies* (New York, 1958), b 121.

Prophets *plus* such other books as the Psalter.[23] Although there was as yet no closed corpus of the Holy Scriptures, such as those ultimately recognized by the Church and Synagogue, there can be no doubt of the fact that the scribal editors and redactors who brought the books of this collectivity into the text-forms now before us in the Hebrew Scriptures—and whose word continued, we must remember, through the several hundred years during which these books (or variant text-forms of these books) were translated into Greek—believed that they were working with sacred materials, texts suffused with or touching upon divine power, and therefore to be handled with the utmost circumspection and care.

The editorial hand is detectable everywhere in the Hebrew Scriptures. It is overt and immediately apparent, of course, in the superscriptions to various groupings of text-material, such as those found at the beginnings of sections of prophecy or of many psalms:

> The burden of Nineveh: the book of the prophetic vision of Nahum the Elkoshite (Nah. 1:1);

> A Psalm of David, when he was in the wilderness of Judah (Ps. 63:1).

Or, though far more rarely and somewhat obscurely, it can be found marking the close of portions of text, as in the following two passages of the Book of Jeremiah:

> Thus far the judgment of Moab (Jer. 48:47)

> "And they grow weary": thus far the words of Jeremiah (Jer. 51:64b).

In the second of these examples, the words in quotation marks—translation of a single word in the Hebrew—consist of a citation of the final word in Jer. 51:58.[24] Our editor is tell-

---

[23] As shown in my paper, "The Qumran Authors' SPR HHGH/Y," *Journal of Near Eastern Studies*, XX (1961), 109-114. Cf. *Cambridge History of the Bible*, I (Cambridge, 1970), 154.

[24] Failure to understand that the quoted words are part of the editorial note has resulted in their omission from the Revised Standard Version and the New English Bible. Older versions inexplicably include the quoted words in Seraiah's incantation (51:64a)

ing us that that word is the final one of Jeremiah's own utterances; verses 51:59-64a (the passage discussed at the end of Chapter Three above), he thus informs us, were not found by him among Jeremiah's own words, but in some other source. We do not know whether that source was included in the text of Jeremiah before our editor. The Septuagint (Greek) version of Jeremiah, it is interesting to note, does not contain our Hebrew 48:47 and 51:64b (for 51:59-64a see the Septuagint's chapter 28). These verses, apparently, were not in the Hebrew text of the Book of Jeremiah that lay before the Greek translator(s), a text which, accordingly, was manifestly different from the one transmitted by the editor of our Hebrew text which, through the Massoretes, has come down to us.

Less overtly, but quite as unmistakably, the editorial or redactional hand has indicated itself to us (a) in a frequently used Hebrew phrase, (b) in a linguistic device specifically adapted to editorial or redactional use, and (c) in a technical term.

The Hebrew phrase is *'adh hay-yōm haz-zeh* "until this day." In many instances of the usage it is clear that "this day" is the day of the compiler or editor of the narrative in which the phrase occurs; and sometimes this enables us to set a terminal date for the redaction of the text-material past which the redaction could not have been done. When, for example, we are told that David was given the city of Ziklag by Achish, king of Gath, and that,

> Therefore Ziklag has belonged to the kings of Judah until this day (I Sam. 27:6),

we realize that "this day" cannot refer to a time later than the fall of the Judean kingdom in 587 B.C.E., hence, that the work of which this narrative is a part must have been edited for use by readers or hearers at some point in time before this date. And when, similarly, we read of the ark of the covenant and its poles that the priests set them under the wings of the cherubim in the inner sanctuary of Solomon's temple,

> and they are there to this day (I Kings 8:8);

we are given to understand that "this day" cannot post-date

the destruction of the temple, and that this portion of I Kings must also have been composed and made available to readers or hearers before 587 B.C.E.

The Biblical Hebrew redactional or editorial device mentioned above consists of the temporal adverb *'āz* ("then," "this was when") followed by a verb-form signifying an incomplete action (the Hebrew imperfect). By means of this device, an additional or supplementary account that refers to a time prior to or concurrent with that of the main account may be introduced into, and made part of, the main text; the scriptural editor is thus enabled to supplement, or add to, the preceding bloc of text-material without having to disrupt or rewrite it. The device always signals and expresses such disproportional post-placement yet temporal priority; it is often resorted to, accordingly, when an editor wishes to introduce additional material from a source extraneous to, or different from, that from which his just-previously set forth bloc of material has been taken or produced. Numbers 21:10 following, for example, is the account of Israel's itinerary from Mount Hor to Moab. Interpolated into this account is the Song of the Well, introduced by our redactional device:

> This was when Israel sang this song: "Spring up, O well!" etc. (Num. 21:17).

The fact that the Song is an interpolation, drawn from another source than that of the previous account is signalled by *'āz* ("this was when") and the immediately following imperfect verb-form *yāshīr* ("sang"). The fact that the verb is an imperfect form indicates that the singing is to be regarded as done during the assembly of the people mentioned in the immediately preceding verse (21:16). Another example of this redactional device is found at the outset of the story of King Solomon's judgment (I Kings 3:16-28):

> This was when two women, harlots, came to the king ... (3:16).

As indicated by employment of our device here, the story, taken by the editor of this part of Kings from another source than that of the immediately preceding bloc of text-material, was considered by him to have taken place at Gibeon (3:5 above), before the king "came to Jerusalem and stood before the ark of the Lord's covenant" (3:15).[25]

The technical term in which the redactional hand is evident is the word $n^e$'*ūm* "utterance of," "declaration of." It occurs well over 300 times in the Hebrew Bible, mostly in the prophetic books, where it is found in all save Habakkuk and Jonah. Except for eleven instances (in six of which Balaam is the "utterer" or "declarer"), the term always occurs before one or other of the divine names: "the declaration of the Lord," "the utterance of the God of Israel," "the declaration of the Lord God of Hosts," etc. $N^e$'*ūm* must be considered a redactional technical term because, when followed by the divine name, it always implies a *paraphrased citation* of the designated divine declaration—an always accurate citation, but not necessarily a meticulously exact *quotation* of the words held to have been uttered by God. The distinction in usage between paraphrased citation ($n^e$'*ūm*) and exact quotation is clearly seen in passages which are composed of divine words couched in both formats. This double format occurs, for example, in the prophecy against Sennacherib, king of Assyria, that Isaiah sent to the Judean king, Hezekiah:

> "Therefore thus says the Lord respecting the king of Assyria: 'He shall not enter this city, nor shoot arrow there, nor confront it with shield, nor cast up siege-ramp against it.' By the way he took in coming shall he go back, and he will not enter this city, is the declaration of the Lord" (Isa. 37:33-34 II Kings 19:32-33).

Here, the exact quotation is introduced by "Therefore thus says ('*āmar*) the Lord," while the paraphrased citation is followed by "is the declaration ($n^e$'*ūm*) of the Lord." We have the same distinction in this famous passage:

---

[25] This redactional device introduces blocs of additional or supplemental text-material at some fifteen places in the Pentateuch and Former Prophets. The existence of the device in Biblical Hebrew is proved, and its functioning demonstrated, in my article, "'*Az* Followed by Imperfect Verb-Form in Preterite Contexts: A Redactional Device in Biblical Hebrew" (*Vetus Testamentum* XXXIV [1984], 53-62).

> "Thus says the Lord: 'Let not the wise man be boastful of
> his wisdom, nor the mighty man of his might; nor the
> wealthy man of his wealth; but let whoever would boast
> be boastful of this, of understanding and of knowing me:
> that I am the Lord, enacter of loving kindness, justice and
> righteousness on earth;' for it is in these matters that I de-
> light, is the declaration of the Lord" (Jer. 9:22-23[23-24]).

And it appears, as well, in the following:

> "Thus says the Lord: 'And the upholders of Egypt shall
> fall, and the exaltation of her power shall go down'; from
> Migdol to Syene shall they fall in her by the sword, is the
> declaration of the Lord God" (Ezek. 30:6).

In two instances (Isa. 56:8 and Ps. 110:1), our technical redactional term occurs at the outset of the thus-indicated paraphrased citation. Quite frequently, especially with a strong
asseveration or oath, it occurs in the middle of the declaration:

> And the angel of the Lord called out to Abraham a second
> time from the heavens, and said: "By myself I have sworn,
> is the declaration of the Lord, that because you have done
> this thing, and have not withheld your son, your only one,
> that I will indeed bless you," etc. (Gen. 22:15-17);

> "Therefore, is the declaration of the Lord God of Israel, I have
> indeed said your house and your father's house would walk
> before me for ever; but now, is the declaration of the Lord, far
> be it from me, for them that honor me will I honor, whereas
> those that despise me shall be disdained" (I Sam. 3:30);

> "But if you do not obey these words, I have sworn by my-
> self, is the declaration of the Lord, that this house shall be-
> come a ruin" (Jer. 22:5);

> "Behold, days are coming, is the declaration of the Lord,
> when I shall make a new covenant with the House of Israel
> and the House of Judah" (Jer. 31:31).

Most commonly, however, *ne'ūm* occurs at the end of the
paraphrased citation:

> The Lord enters a legal disputation with the elders of his
> people and their princes: "—and it is you who have
> burned out the vineyard; the robbed spoil of the poor is in
> your houses." By what right do you crush my people, and
> grind the faces of the poor? is the declaration of the Lord
> God of Hosts (Isa. 3:14-15);

> Is it that I am a God near at hand, but not a God far off? is
> the declaration of the Lord; Or can a man covertly conceal
> himself without my seeing him? is the declaration of the
> Lord; Do I not fill heaven and earth? is the declaration of
> the Lord (Jer. 23:23-24);

> "And I will put my spirit in you, and you shall love again,
> and I will set you upon your own ground"; and you shall
> know that it is I, the Lord, who have spoken and enacted
> it, is the declaration of the Lord (Ezek. 37:14).

The editorial hand is nowhere in the Scriptures more clearly attested by the contents of the texts than in the four major bodies of "literary prophecy," the books of Isaiah, Jeremiah, Ezekiel and The Twelve (the so-called "minor prophets"). The fact that ancient editors and redactors produced these books as we now find them before us in the Hebrew Bible is plainly and ineluctably evident as soon as we notice the variegated nature of their contents, the many different kinds of textual material out of which they have editorially and redactionally been constituted as they now are. There are four main classes of these kinds of material:

  (1) autobiographical accounts—dictated or written by the prophets themselves—of prophetic experiences, colloquies with other persons, visions, and actions;

  (2) biographical accounts, by witnesses or tradents, of what the prophets did and said;

  (3) utterances, by the prophets, of directly quoted, paraphrased, or prophetically interpreted and presented, words of God; and

  (4) historical narratives in which the prophets figure, in part duplicating or supplementing narratives found in II Kings and II Chronicles.

Very striking is the fact that both autobiographical and biographical accounts of a particular prophet's deeds and words are editorially brought together within the same corpus of prophetic material. Isaiah 6:1 and 8:1, for example, introduce autobiographical accounts by the prophet, whereas 7:3, 20:2 and 37:21 introduce biographically couched state-

ments. Jeremiah's commissioning as prophet (1:4f.) is autobiographical, as are 11:6f., 13:1f. and many other passages,
while at 20:2f., 25:1f., 29:1f., and often, we find biographical
reports. The editorial hand in this prophetic corpus is
perhaps plainest in evidence in the many places where, as in
Jer. 32:1f., the material is first couched as a biographical
account, and then (32:6f.) moves into a body of autobiographical material. Practically all the accounts of Ezekiel's prophetic
experience are autobiographical. Yet here too, following the
autobiographically presented 1:1, we have the biographical
statement in 1:3. Except for the incidental mention of the
name "Ezekiel" in a speech of the Lord (at 24:24), the
biographical reference in 1:3—probably by the first redactor
of our Book of Ezekiel—is our sole source for the fact that the
prophetic protagonist of this extraordinary text-corpus was
"Ezekiel the priest, the son of Buzi."

Although the editorial hand in the prophetic corpora is
perhaps most clearly noticeable in the collocation of autobiographical materials, it is not the lives and personalities of the
prophets themselves that is at the center of the editors' and
redactors' concern, but the creative and corrective words and
will of God—the constituent forces of the world's realities,
as they believed, sent by God into the world through the
agency and mediacy of the prophets. The historical narratives of the prophetic books, apart from accounts of non-
verbal prophetic actions such as the performance of "sign
and portents," are included in the books because they
"witness" and corroborate the prophetically mediated
divine words and other indications of divine will. Primacy
of importance among the several classes of material included
in the prophetic books is thus editorially accorded to the
divine words uttered by the prophets. Next in importance
are the accounts of those aspects of prophetic experience
clearly revelatory of the divine will in some regard. And
finally, though subordinated in importance to the rest, is the
historical "witness"-material. At the heart of the editors' and
redactors' concern in assembling and presenting our prophetic
books is the word-action of God—preferably as historically
attested and corroborated—through and with an errant and

refractory mankind (commencing with Israel) to achieve realization of his covenanted scheme of a divine-human-natural world-order.

As history, from the standpoint of the ancient Israelite editors and redactors of the Hebrew Scriptures, is realized or fulfilled prophecy, while prophecy is the word-essence or presage of historical reality (existent or yet-to-be), the presence together of both kinds of text-material in the prophetic books is only what the earliest readers and hearers of these texts would expect. Indeed there is evidence in the Scriptures themselves, especially in the titles of books mentioned by the author of Chronicles, of an even closer connection between historical and prophetic text-material than that which now obtains in our books of literary prophecy. Of King Solomon, for example, the Chronicler writes:

> Now the rest of Solomon's acts, the early ones and the later, are they not written in *The Words of Nathan the Prophet*, and in *The Prophecy of Ahijah the Shilonite*, and in *The Visioning of Iddo the Seer concerning Jeroboam the Son of Nebat*? (II Chr. 9:29).

Besides other sources—including, as we know, such historical words as our scriptural I Kings—the Chronicler thus informs us that he drew his account of the historical facts of Solomon's reign from the three books of prophecy mentioned by title in this verse. These books, accordingly, contained not only prophetic text-material, but such factual historical narratives as their authors considered pertinent and relevant to the recorded prophecies.

Toward the end of his account of King Jehoshaphat's reign, again, the Chronicler tells us:

> Now the rest of Jehoshaphat's acts, the early ones and the later, behold, they are written in *The Words of Jehu Son of Hanani*, which was included in *The Books of the Kings of Israel* (II Chr. 20:34).

According to this note, a prophetic work which contained an historical account of Jehoshaphat's career as king of Judah was itself incorporated in a book that was primarily an historical work. The relationship between prophetical and historical text-material was such, judging by the testimony of a writer who plainly knew the contents of the works he cites, that a book primarily of prophecy would naturally include history, while a book intended primarily as a history could include the words of prophecy which were the first adumbrations of the subsequently realized historical events. The prophet Isaiah, indeed, is said by the Chronicler to have been the author of an account of the reign of King Uzziah:

> Now the rest of the acts of Uzziah, the early ones and the later, the prophet Isaiah, son of Amoz, wrote (II Chr. 26:22).

Another note of the Chronicler's has relevance for the redaction of our scriptural books of II Kings and of Isaiah:

> Now the rest of the acts of Hezekiah, and his acts of faithful love, behold, they are written in *The Vision of the Prophet Isaiah Son of Amoz*, in *The Book of the Kings of Judah and Israel* (II Chr. 32:32).

The superscription of our scriptural book of Isaiah begins, we recall, "The Vision of Isaiah son of Amoz ...," and Chapters 36-39 of this prophetic book consist of an account of Hezekiah's reign; these chapters are duplicated in slightly variant form, and with omission of Hezekiah's written prayer for recovery from illness (38:9-20), in II Kings 18:13-20 (and cf. II Chr. 32:20-33). As they are now before us in the Hebrew Bible, both II Kings and Isaiah have a section consisting of "the acts of Hezekiah," but each book is a separate entity. Available to the Chronicler, however, was a single work, *The Book of the Kings of Judah and Israel*, which incorporated a book entitled *The Vision of the Prophet Isaiah Son of Amoz*, in which, just as in our present scriptural Isaiah, appeared an account of "the acts of Hezekiah and his acts of faithful love."

The Chronicler tells us of still other works which combined prophecy and history, or which may even have been written by prophets or seers; see, for examples, I Chr. 29:29, II Chr. 12:15, 13:22 and 33:19. The text-material now before us in our books of Kings and in Isaiah and Jeremiah, in other words, was certainly before the Chronicler (350-300

B.C.E.?) in a multiplicity of variant editions and redactions. In all these works, however variantly the text-material was ordered and redacted, the prophetic content unquestionably consisted of the word-form or "sign"-form of the divine creation or correction of historical reality, while the historical parts comprised the "witness"-fulfillment of the divine word or sign. In our scriptural Book of Isaiah, for example, the account of Hezekiah's reign (Chapters 36-39) appears as an historical attestation of a salvation that was created by a divine utterance sent into the world through the prophet. Hence it is editorially placed in the Book where it might best serve as an assurance to readers and hearers that the thus-far unrealized divine promises of Israel's restoration and key-role in the coming great scheme of divine-human-natural world-order—the promise foretold, argued, interpreted, and prayed for especially in Chapters 34-35 and 40-66—was certainly as well known to the ancient editors and redactors who brought this corpus of prophecy-plus-history together as it is clear to us today. To those editors and redactors, however, the true "author" of the prophetic matter, the true creator of the corroborative history, was God. The exact personal identity of the prophetic mediators of those divine word-acts and fulfillments—whether Isaiah himself, or one or more of his disciples—was a matter of far less significance and importance. Of overriding and guiding importance to the editors and redactors who brought the books of the Hebrew Bible into their present textual disposition and format was their conviction that these books constituted the word-essence—"witnessed," corroborated, prayed for in various ways—of the world's reality as intended by God.

## 2. The Ordering and Sequence of Texts Containing "Holy Words"

Because the books of the Hebrew Bible, especially of the Pentateuch and the Prophets ("the Law and the Prophets"), contained God's creating and correcting words, they were regarded by the ancient Israelite editors and redactors who brought them together as we have them, and by their fellow-Israelite readers and hearers, as *holy books*, their divine words as *holy words*. This means, as pointed out above (Chapter

One, §4), that the texts of these words were considered
instruments of power, instrumentalities capable of bringing
good or inflicting evil upon those who might come into
contact with them—those handling, reading or hearing
them—depending upon the state of readiness to absorb their
power of those in such contact. In preparing books containing holy words, accordingly, the editors and redactors set
out and ordered the text-materials at their disposal in such
manner as they deemed might least expose themselves and
their covenant-loyal Israelite readers and hearers to harm
and might most make for their weal and good fortune: might
defend them against curse and open them to blessing.

Their effort to avoid or nullify the risks of personal
endangerment involved in the presentation of divine words
led the editors and redactors of such holy texts to set them
out in an order and sequence which often appears to modern
western readers utterly bizarre, anomalous, inchoate to the
point of incoherence. It was not that the ancient scribal
editors and redactors were insensitive to such compositional
virtues as coherence, clarity, logical order, and the like, but
rather that they subordinated such excellencies of rhetoric
and style to their anxiety to minimize the risks involved in
the presentation of holy texts and their zeal to promote the
welfare of covenant-loyal Israel. Our editors and redactors
were manifestly concerned to avoid exposure to two main
categories of risk vis-à-vis holy words: (1) the risk that a
reader or hearer might be misled into believing that a divine
word had turned out to be false; (2) the risk involved in
unmitigated exposure to divine words of threat and punishment. To avoid an impression of possible falsity in a divine
word, an editor could disrupt a coherent and logical sequence
of prophetic statements in order to intrude matter effectively
denying the imputation of divine errancy; to allow such an
impression lodgement even momentarily in the soul of a
reader or hearer might cause an irreparable breach in that
soul. And again, persons exposed to contact with divine
words of destruction—words aimed at the group of which
the readers or hearers were members—might find themselves overtaken by the damage projected by the words

unless the threat of such words could be off-set by other divine words carrying assurance of group-welfare. Hence, in our books of literary prophecy, we find abrupt and sudden alternations between blocs of text-material promising threat and destruction to the people of God's covenant, and blocs of material promising them weal and salvation—alternations, of course, quite subversive of our modern literary notions of compositional unity and coherence. Following are examples of both kinds of editorially induced "anomaly."

In the latter part of the Book of Amos, four prophetic visions—7:1-3, 7:4-6, 7:7-9 and 8:1-3—are set out in a particular order. In the case of the first two visions, threatened disaster by locust-plague and by fire respectively are successfully averted through prayer and intercession by the prophet; in the third, an impending negative judgment of the uprightness of north Israel, declared undivertable, is on the point of being introduced into the people's midst, in consequence of which Israel's sanctuaries and the ruling house of Jeroboam would be destroyed; and in the fourth, the time of the destruction of the north Israelite people and of their kings is declared at hand. Between the close of the third vision, which concludes with the Lord's statement,

> "... and I shall rise up against the House of Jeroboam with the sword" (Amos 7:9),

and the opening of the fourth vision (8:1f.), a bloc of narrative material has deliberately, abruptly, and without expressed explanation, been intruded. This narrative material (7:10-17) begins as follows:

> Then Amaziah, the priest of Bethel, sent to Jeroboam, the king of Israel, saying, "Amos has framed a conspiracy against you inside the House of Israel, and the land is not able to endure all his words. For thus has Amos said: 'By the sword shall Jeroboam die, and Israel shall certainly be exiled away from its terrain'" (7:10-11).

Continuing with an interesting colloquy between Amaziah and Amos, in which Amos denies that his livelihood is gained from professional prophesying, the interpolated bloc of narrative material closes with a dire prophetic threat

against Amaziah and his family and a reassertion of the
certainty of Israel's impending exile.

This narrative about Amaziah and Amos, wherever it
was placed in the corpus of Amos-material originally at the
disposal of the editor who produced our present book, has
now been intruded between the third and fourth visions
because the prophecy against "the House of Jeroboam" at the
end of the third vision effectively rebuts and denies the allegation, by Amaziah, that Amos had prophesied the death of
Jeroboam "by the sword." As cited by Amaziah in the narrative, Amos' prophecy against Jeroboam was known by the
editor to be false: it was not Jeroboam himself who died by
the sword, but his son Zechariah who died in this way (cf. II
Kings 14:29, 15:10). If, then, the Amaziah-Amos narrative
was to be included in *The Words of Amos* (and it was obviously
too important to omit), Amaziah's citation of Amos' predic-
tion—known not to have come true—could not be left to
stand in its original place in the text, where it might tempt
readers and hearers to think that here was a divine word that
had gone unfulfilled. To allow the citation to stand in such
a place would be to put readers and hearers in jeopardy of
an outbreak of divine wrath—such an outbreak, one might
add, as ought fittingly overtake Israel's sinful evil-doers (few
of whom would be reading or hearing this prophetic book),
but not covenant-loyal heeders of Israelite literary prophecy.
Never mind that intrusion of the bloc of narrative containing
the misquoted divine word disrupts the succession of the
visions and demolishes its rhetorical effect. The more serious
consideration was given precedence: with the actual divine
word, no faithful Israelite hearer or reader could harbor the
perilous suspicion that a divine word had been sent into the
world through a true prophet, Amos, yet had not been literally fulfilled as it ought properly to have been. "The House
of Jeroboam" could now be understood to have meant
Zechariah, Jeroboam's son and successor, not Jeroboam
himself; and Amaziah, given the lie in the matter of the
misquoted divine word, could be seen as one who had
lodged a characteristically false accusation against Amos
with the king. The awe inspired by the Lord's words and the

precautions to be taken in the handling of such holy words,
the awe and the precautions which have resulted in the liter-
arily anomalous disruption of this section of *The Words of
Amos*, are, in effect, a carrying-out of the instructions regarding prophets and their words found at Deut. 18:17-22 and
already cited above (Chapter One, §4).

In ordering and arranging the books of Israelite prophecy, the editors and redactors acted in full consciousness of
their conviction that they themselves, as well as all other
readers and hearers, were being brought into physical and
psychical contact with so many power-concentrates of the
most tremendous force in the universe: the holy words of
God. They were handling, and exposing others to, the power-
fraught word-essence-acts of an Author self-characterized as

> "Former of light and creator of darkness,
> Maker of weal and creator of woe,
> I, the Lord, am doer of all these" (Isa. 45:7).

None could tell when an as yet unfulfilled divine word-act
might begin to be realized. Hence a word of threatened
"woe" was perilous to persons identifiable as among those
against whom the threat was uttered, even though such
persons might be undeserving of having the threat visited
upon them. But "weal"-words for the deserving were also at
hand, and these, properly placed, could shield them from
being overcome by the words of "woe."

The 30th chapter of the Book of Jeremiah, for example,
contains a divine proclamation of the mortal wound visited
upon Israel and Judah in chastisement of their sins:

> For thus says the Lord:
> "Your fracture is incurable,
> your wounds devastating;
> none judges your case as curable,
> healing medicaments have you none.
> All your lovers have forgotten you,
> they do not seek you out,
> for I have struck you as an enemy strikes,
> a cruel foe's chastising;
> because your iniquity was great,
> your sins waxed many.
> Why cry out against your fracture?

Your anguish is incurable:
because your iniquity was great,
your sins waxed many,
I have done these things to you" (Jer. 30:12-15).

The injury done to Israel and Judah we note is irreparable: the word-form of this divinely intended reality-to-be is the adumbration of the approaching demise of these organized polities. Yet immediately following this grim prognostic we have a divine assurance that the wounds visited upon Israel and Judah are not mortal, not incurable, but are to be healed:

"Therefore all that devour you shall be devoured,
and all, all your foes shall go into captivity;
your despoilers shall become spoil,
and all your plunderers shall I set for plunder.
For I will bring restored health up for you,"
and I will heal you of your wounds, is the
    declaration of the Lord,
because they have called you an outcast:
"Zion, she whom none seeks out" (Jer. 30:16-17).

These two passages have editorially been brought into immediately successive proximity because the promised "healing" of the second directly contradicts and off-sets the threatened "incurable fracture" and imminent demise of the first. The two passages were plainly not originally thus successive: this is shown by the glaringly illogical "therefore" at the outset of the second passage, and by the fact that the "plunderers" and "despoilers" of the latter are obviously not the forgetful "lovers" of the first. If, then, the two passages have deliberately been brought together, this is because the editor(s) have here subordinated rhetorically logical consistency to their desire to off-set threat by promise: only God, it was obviously believed, could heal an otherwise "devastating" and "incurable" wound. This belief, indeed, is plainly stated as a divine word to Jeremiah:

For thus says the Lord: "Just as I have brought on this people all this great disaster, so it is I who am going to bring upon them all the good which I am pronouncing upon them" (Jer. 32:42).

Further assurance of the non-fatality of the "incurable fracture" that has overtaken Israel is contained in the divine statement—repeated in a different context elsewhere in the book (46:28)—that immediately precedes the first of our two passages:

> "For I will make a full end in the case of all the nations whither I have scattered you; but of you I will not make a full end. I shall, however, chastise you according to justice, and not let you off scot-free" (Jer. 30:11).

As the power-laden divine utterances of our two passages are now editorially arranged, those readers and hearers who deserved to survive the catastrophe inflicted upon justly chastised Israel could feel free of the jeopardy involved in the words of disaster, and could look forward to the blessings involved in the words of weal.

Passages of "holy words," so juxtaposed in redaction as to off-set their threats of woe by their promises of weal, occur relatively frequently in the prophetic literature. The punishment and suffering which are to assail a sinful Israel and Jerusalem, as depicted in the first chapter of Isaiah, are immediately followed by the second chapter's depiction (repeated in a slightly variant version at Micah 4:1-4) of the redeemed and blessed future Zion to which, as the center and fountain-head of world peace, all the nations would advert. In Hosea, the threatened destruction and divine casting-off of the people of northern Israel portrayed in 1:2-8 is at once followed by the promised recovery and restoration of 2:1-2 (1:10-11). The textual material in Micah, it may be pointed out, is so ordered that sections of text prognostic of woe are alternated with blocs of material predictive of weal: thus chapters 1-3 proclaim woe, 4:1-5:8(9) weal; 5:9(10)-7:6 woe, 7:7-20 weal. No book of Israelite prophecy, indeed, may consist solely of doom and threatened disasters. Even if, as in Ezekiel's famous vision (chapter 37), "the whole house of Israel" should be so utterly destroyed as to consist entirely of dead, dry bones, they were to be restored to life:

> "Thus says the Lord God: 'Behold, it is I who, opening your graves, shall raise you up out of your graves, O my people; and I will bring you to the land of Israel. And you

will know that it is I, the Lord, when, opening your graves
and raising you up out of your graves, O my people, I put
my spirit in you so that you live again, and I set you down
upon your soil.' Then you will know that it is I, the Lord,
who have spoken word, and performed it, is the declaration of the Lord" (Ezek. 37:12-14).

A "holy word" of disaster would indeed, in the belief of
the redactors and editors of our prophetic texts, usher the
predicted overthrow into the world. But those editors and
redactors were careful to indicate the exact dimensions of the
disaster where they could, to bring out its precise limits and,
where necessary, to place alongside an off-setting contrary
utterance. In an oracle adverting to the "people of Israel," we
find this remarkable passage:

> Behold, the eyes of the Lord God are upon the sinful king-
> dom, "—and I shall destroy it off the face of the earth—"
> except that I shall assuredly not destroy the House of Jacob,
> is the declaration of the Lord (Amos 9:8).

The *kingdom* of north Israel, the organized polity, it is here
emphasized, was to be destroyed, but the "House of Jacob,"
the *peoplehood* of Israel, was to survive the destruction of that
organized political structure. Underlying the seemingly
bizarre collocation of absolute threat and off-setting contrary
qualification is the assumption of the editor(s) that "holy
words" have the power of God in them: "holy words" are as
capable of working ill or good upon those in contact with
them as any other object or instrumentality filled with divine
power. Just as contact with the holy Ark of the Lord, however
inadvertent and well-intentioned, brought death to poor
Uzzah, while it brought felicity and blessing to Obed-edom
the Gittite and all his household (II Samuel 6:6-11), so "holy
words" were capable of blasting or blessing their hearers and
readers. Responsible editors and redactors, accordingly,
would so order the "holy words" in their charge as to
promote blessing and impede disaster.

For our part as modern western readers, realizing that
such a purpose as that described above was among the chief
concerns of those who brought the texts of our books of scriptural prophecy into their present format, we begin to miti-

gate our bewilderment and distress—born of our own modern assumptions and expectations as to the literary art —at those texts' fragmentedness, confused order, seeming inconsistency, and bizarre incoherence.

## 3. Conflation of Texts

As suggested above, the ancient editors and redactors who brought the books of the Hebrew Bible into the text-forms in which they are now before us—books, we must not forget, which to them and to countless others after them were *holy*—found the text-material which they thus reordered and reworked available in a multiplicity of variant formats and arrangements. Unquestionably, too, our editors and redactors often confronted more than one manuscript of the self-same body of text-material, handwritten copies of the same work which—as inevitably occurs in the course of manu-script-transmission—must have exhibited variation in word -choice, word-order, statement-attribution, inclusion or abridg-ment of details, and other matters of style. A modern critical editor, confronting such variation in the written witnesses at his disposal to the text he is trying to establish, will select that one of the variant possibilities which he judges to be correct and present it in his main text; the rejected variants will be exhibited in an *"apparatus criticus"* at the foot of the page carrying the main text. Our ancient editors and redactors, unwilling or not daring, in the case of a book which they believed to be holy, to determine the "true" reading and to set the other possibilities aside, frequently took care to preserve the variants by incorporating them into the main text itself. Where, that is to say, they found two or more slightly variant readings in their manuscript-sources, they often would fuse them into a composite reading; hence the conflation of many passages of the Hebrew Scriptures.

It is to such conflation—to the desires of the editors and redactors to preserve the variants in the manuscripts from which they constituted the main text—that some composi-tional effects which to us seem strange and even anomalous are directly attributable. Many instances of these bizarreries and anomalies, it should perhaps be added, are concealed by the efforts of modern translators to produce readable texts. As the following representative examples show, however, any alert reader will be able to note the fact, and to observe the consequences, of such conflation in the Hebrew Bible.

At Gen. 23:1, for example, the King James Version reads,

> And Sarah was an hundred and seven and twenty years old: *these were* the years of the life of Sarah.

The words "*these were*" are here italicized, as is standard practice in the KJV, in order to alert the reader to the fact that the words so printed do not translate words of the original Hebrew text, but have been inserted by the translators to abate the awkwardness, in English, of a more literal render-ing of the Hebrew verse. Later editions and some revisions of the KJV omit the italics of "these were" and thus obscure the fact that the two words represent nothing in the Hebrew text. The New English Bible (1970), finally, simply omits "*these were* the years of the life of Sarah"—even with "*these were*" in italics, the statement is only too obviously redun-dant—and joins the first half of verse 2 to the first half of verse 1:

> [1]Sarah lived for a hundred and twenty-seven years, [2]and died in Kiriath-arba, which is Hebron, in Canaan.

The explanation of the awkward redundancy of Gen. 23:1 is quite simple. Before the editor(s) who produced the verse as we now find it were two manuscripts, one of which read,

> [1]And the life of Sarah was a hundred and twenty-seven years, [2]and then Sarah died ....

while the other read,

> [1]And the years of Sarah's life were a hundred and twenty-seven years, [2]and then Sarah died ....

(The word "life" in Hebrew is plural in form, hence the verb in both manuscript-texts was alike also plural.) In order to preserve the slightly variant reading "the years of Sarah's life" alongside the simpler "the life of Sarah," the editor(s) placed the former at the end of the sentence comprised by verse 1—at the foot of the verse instead of at the foot of the page, as a modern editor of a critically edited text would do—and thus produced our now conflate text of this verse. Both readings, it should perhaps be added, are in quite idiomatic Biblical Hebrew; compare, for "the years of Sarah's life," the similar instances at Exod. 6:16, 18, and 20.

Another example of conflation-induced redundancy is found at Exod. 6:26-27, where the King James Version reads,

> [26]These *are* that Aaron and Moses, to whom the Lord said, Bring out the children of Israel from the land of Egypt according to their armies.

> [27]These *are* they which spoke to Pharaoh king of Egypt, to bring out the children of Israel from Egypt: these *are* that Moses and Aaron.

The final words of verse 27 are precisely the same as the opening words of verse 26, save that the names "Aaron" and "Moses" have switched positions: it is "Aaron and Moses" in verse 26, but "Moses and Aaron" at the end of verse 27. Here again the editor(s) have conflated two variant manuscript-readings; in one the order of the names in the opening words was "Aaron and Moses," in the other the passage opened with "Moses and Aaron." What now seems to us a strange redundancy in the text was born of the desire of the editor(s) to preserve and to transmit both readings.

Similarly conflate in Num. 7:89:

> And when Moses entered the tent of meeting in order to speak with him [=the Lord], he heard the voice speaking to him from above the propitiation-slab which was over the ark of the testimony, from between the two cherubim: and it spoke to him.

At this point where one manuscript-source before the editor(s) read "... the voice speaking to him ...," another read "... the voice, and it spoke to him ..."; here again the alternative reading has been preserved at the end of the verse, and has thus engendered the seemingly needless and bizarre repetition of an already stated detail.

Rather more extensive is the manuscript-source variation underlying, and from which has been constituted, our presently conflate text of I Sam. 4:21-22:

> [21]And she named the boy Ichabod, saying, "Glory has de-
> parted from Israel," with regard to the capture of the ark
> of God and with regard to her father-in-law and her hus-
> band.
>
> [22]And she said, "Glory has departed from Israel," because
> the ark of God had been captured.

That the text of this passage is conflate is clear from the fact
that the content of verse 22, except for three instances of
slight verbal variation, has already been stated (along with
additional details) in verse 21. The three variant readings are:
"saying"/"And she said," "with regard to"/"because," "the
capture of"/"had been captured." The manuscript-version from
which verse 22 was drawn unquestionably contained the
words "And she named the boy Ichabod," but either made
no mention of the father-in-law and the husband, or else
referred to them in the identical words of their mention in v.
21. We note that text-conflation in order to preserve variant
readings was confined to the minimum amount necessary to
exhibit the actual variants, and that the editor(s) saw no
reason to record the fact that a particular manuscript-source
did not contain the material from an alternative source that
had already been presented.

It was the preservation of variant holy words, as these
were expressly stated in an alternative manuscript-source,
not merely the noting of such differences between manuscript-sources as that one abridged where another did not,
that concerned the editors and redactors of these sacred
texts. This is the consideration, plainly, which explains the
intrusive insertion of Exod. 15:20-21—

> [20]Then Miriam the prophetess, Aaron's sister, took timbrel
> in hand, and all the women came out after her, with tim-
> brels and in dance.
>
> [21]And Miriam sang to them: "Sing ye to the Lord, for he
> has risen up gloriously; horse and rider has he cast into the
> sea"

—at the end of the passage which contains the Song at the

Sea (Exod. 15:1-9). As shown by the use, pointed out above of redactional '*āz* and the imperfect verb-form *yāshīr* ("This was when Moses and the Israelites sang this song ..."), the Song, as cited, was drawn from another manuscript-source than that followed in the immediately preceding bloc of text-material (14:26-31). The latter also contained the Song, but in this source the introductory words were those we now find in our text intruded at its end: verses 20-21, as cited above (possibly ending with the words "and they said, namely," as at the end of 15:1a). We have corroborative evidence of the fact that these verses are the now displaced, variant intro-duction to the Song that once stood in the manuscript-version from which 14:26-31 was drawn. Since the original Hebrew grammatical form of the prepositional phrase "to them" in verse 21 includes the masculine-plural pronoun (*lāhem*), its antecedent cannot be "the women" of verse 20, in which case the feminine-plural pronoun would be required (*lāhen*). The antecedent of the masculine-plural pronoun is, in fact, the "Israel" of 14:31; and since this is the case, we real-ize that 15:20-21 are intrusive where they now stand and are displaced from where they must once have stood in the manuscript-version from which our editor(s) took them. It was because the editor(s) thus deliberately took care to preserve the variant introduction that stood in this manu-script-version—the version to which 14:26-31 belonged—that we now find this alternative introduction in 15:20-21, displaced to the end of the Song.

In the Latter Prophets, doublets of material that were substantially variant were usually placed by the editor(s) at widely separate points within the contents of a given book. However, editorial use has also been made of the technique of verse-conflation in order to preserve slighter textual vari-ants. Thus, at Jeremiah 38:17, we have the following awkwardly redundant text:

> Then Jeremiah said to Zedekiah, "Thus says the Lord, God of Hosts, God of Israel: 'If you will definitely go out to the commanders of the king of Babylon, then you personally shall live, and this city shall not be burned with fire; then you and your house shall live.'"

In one of the two (at least) manuscripts at the disposal of the editor(s) this verse read "... then you personally shall live, and this city shall not be burned with fire"; in another, ... then you and your house shall live, and this city shall not be burned with fire."

Conflated variant readings, similarly, underlie the orotund present text of Jeremiah 42:5-6:

> [5]And they, for their part, said to Jeremiah, "May the Lord be a true and faithful witness against us if we do not act in strict accord with the whole of the word which the Lord your God may send you regarding us.

> [6]Whether for good or for ill, the voice of the Lord our God to whom we are sending you we will obey; so that it will go well with us, because we will obey the voice of the Lord our God."

Verse 6 in one of the two manuscripts before our editor(s) here ended with "... we will obey," and did not contain the final statement, "so that it will go well," etc. In the other manuscript, all the first part of verse 6, "Whether for good or for ill ... we will obey" was omitted, and the final statement followed directly upon the close of verse 5: "... regarding us, so that it will go well with us because we obey the voice of the Lord our God."

In Ezekiel, editorial interest in preserving textual variants was sufficiently strong to result in the conflation of alternative grammatical forms; the conflated resultant words are linguistically impossible in Biblical Hebrew. One such instance is the word $w^e n\bar{e}'sh^a'ar$ (as it is Massoretically vocalized) at Ezek. 9:8. This grammatical gibberish is a compound of two forms: (1) $w^e nish'\bar{a}r$ (a participle), and (2) $w\bar{a}'eshsh\bar{a}'\bar{e}r$ (a finite verb-form). One manuscript before the editor(s) here read, "And it came to pass, as they were smiting, that I, being left alone [participle], fell upon my face," etc. The other read, "And it came to pass, as they were smiting, that I was left alone [finite verb-form], whereupon I fell upon my face," etc. Another such instance is the phrase translated by the King James Version "and they worshipped" (Revised Standard Version: "worshipping"; New English Bible: "prostrating themselves") at Ezek. 8:16. Here the Hebrew reads $w^e h\bar{e}m\bar{a}$ $mishtah^a w\bar{\imath}them$, a grammatically impossible combination of words. If we resolve the conflated phrase, however, we obtain two perfectly correct word-combinations: (1) $w^eh\bar{e}m\bar{a}$ $mishtah^aw\bar{\iota}m$ ("and they were worshipping"); (2) $w^eh\bar{e}m$ $hishtah^aw\bar{a}y\bar{a}tham$ ("And as for them, their worshipping was …"). In order to make sense, of course, any modern translation of such passages must opt for one or the other of such now conflated readings.

That the Chariot Vision of the first chapter of Ezekiel was before the editor(s) in two slightly variant manuscript-versions is clear from verses 20 and 21. As now fused together, these verses read:

> [20]Wheresoever the spirit was to go, they [= the living creatures] would go, thither the spirit to go, and wheels would be lifted up alongside them, for the spirit of the living creature was in the wheels.
>
> [21]With their going they would go, and with their stopping they would stop, and with their being lifted up off the earth, the wheels would be lifted up alongside them, for the spirit of the living creature was in the wheels.

Analysis of this patently conflate text allows us to see that the one manuscript-version was worded thus:

> [20]Wheresoever the spirit was to go, they would go thither, and the wheels would be lifted up alongside them, for the spirit of the living creature was in the wheels.
>
> [21]With their going they would go, and with their stopping they would stop, and with their being lifted up off the earth they would be lifted up.

The other manuscript-version read as follows:

> [20]Whithersoever the spirit was to go, they would go, while as for the wheels, [21]with their going they would go, and with their stopping they would stop, and with their being lifted up off the earth, the wheels would be lifted up alongside them, for the spirit of the living creature was in the wheels.

Consideration of the double format of entire sections and chapters of the text of Ezekiel, as well as the frequent instances of conflate readings and other remarkable features of the text, makes it virtually certain that the manuscript-versions from which the editor(s) produced the work as we now have it comprised two separate editions of the book, each perhaps issued at different times by the prophet himself.

Recognized as a holy book centuries before the destruction of the Second Temple in 70 C.E., the Psalter, too, exhibits conflate readings. The final four verses of Psalm 24, for example, now appear as follows:

> [7]Lift up your heads, O gates,
> and be lifted up, O everlasting doors,
> that the King of glory may come in.
>
> [8]Who now is the King of glory?
> The Lord, strong and mighty,
> The Lord, mighty in battle.
>
> [9]Lift up your heads, O gates,
> and lift up the everlasting doors,
> that the King of glory may come in.
>
> [10]Who is he now, the King of glory?
> The Lord of Hosts, he is the King of Glory. *Selah.*

Two slightly variant texts of the final verses of this Psalm have here been conflated. One originally consisted of verses 7, 8, and 10b; the other was comprised of 9, 10a, 8bc and 10b. The conflation, while preserving the variant readings, has been artfully arranged with an eye to retaining as much of the original poetic form as possible.

At Psalm 130:6, to point out a final example, we have the following conflate text:

> My soul waits for the Lord
> more than watchmen for the morning,
> O watchmen for the morning.

The awkward redundancy, disguised in various ways by our modern translations, has arisen from the desire of the editor(s) to preserve two slightly variant texts of the Psalm at this point:

> (a)  My soul waits for the Lord
>      more than watchmen for the morning.

(b)  My soul waits for the Lord
     O watchmen for the morning.

Verse-conflation in the books of the Hebrew Bible, as sufficiently shown by the small group of examples presented above, is the consequence of the ancient Israelite editors' efforts to present their sacred texts with word-for-word accuracy. This effort, alongside the attempt to present the holy words of the texts in such sequence and order as to promote blessing and impeded disaster, has resulted in an array of literary effects that quite patently defy and contradict the conceptions and assumptions as to the literary art of our modern western cultures. But if we approach these texts and their holy words while keeping in mind the ancient Israelite beliefs and convictions—especially as to the nature and powers of such words—held by the scribal editors and redactors who brought the books of the Hebrew Bible into their present format, we shall find ourselves able to understand the "strange" and "uncouth" literary phenomena in which these works abound, and better able to appreciate the beauty and grandeur of this ancient scholarly achievement.

# CHAPTER FIVE

## THE NATURE AND FUNCTION OF
## *THE BOOK OF THE UPRIGHT*:
### AN ANCIENT LITERARY FORERUNNER
### OF THE HEBREW BIBLE

The two references in the Former Prophets to *Sēpher Hayyāshār* ("The Book of the Upright," "The Book of the Jasher" [or "Jashar"]) comprise a fact that is in itself of no little importance: they are unimpeachable testimony that a book so titled was in existence before Josh. 10:13 and II Sam. 1:18 were written, and was available as a source for the portions of the Bible of which these passages are intrinsically a part. The ancient Israelite authors, editors and redactors who produced the Book of Joshua and of II Samuel, as these works are now before us in the Scriptures, quite plainly took for granted that the book they called *The Book of the Upright* had come into existence long before their time, and that this book was available to such leaders of the people of Israel as Joshua son of Nun, Moses' successor, and David son of Jesse, who was later to become king. The better our knowledge of this ancient book, therefore, the more clearly we realize how it was perceived by its producers and users, the more likely we are to achieve improved understanding of the nature, genesis and functioning of some of the oldest literature of the Hebrew Bible.

Now the whole of our evidence for what must have been the character and contents of *The Book of the Upright* (hereinafter also: SH = *Sēpher Hayyāshār*) is unfortunately confined to the contexts of the two passages in which the book is named.[26] And since, as will here be demonstrated, these two

---

[26] A third citation of *Sēpher Hayyāshār* has been seen by many scholars in the emendation first proposed by J. Wellhausen (cf. S. R. Driver, *Introduction to the Literature of the Old Testament* [New York, 1914], 192) of the Hebrew text supposed to underlie a reading of the Septuagint at I Kings 8:53a. The underlying premise of this emendation—hereinafter shown to be untenable—is the belief that *The Book of the Upright* consisted solely of poetry.

crucial passages have not been accurately interpreted, we still have no clear conception of the kind of book SH was, nor have we been able to discern its significance for our understanding of the literature of ancient Israel. This chapter, accordingly, will try to correct the long-standing misconception of the character of this ancient book, so that a juster grasp of its true importance for the theory and practice of literature in ancient Israel may be achieved.

I

The prevailing view of SH holds that it was a collection of ancient Hebrew poetry that included, at the very least, both the verses on the stoppage of the sun and moon in Josh. 10:12-13 and those of David's lament over Saul and Jonathan in II Sam. 1:17-27.[27] Some scholars refer to the collection as an "anthology" of poetic selections whose unifying theme was the celebration of ancient Israel's heroes and their deeds; other scholars, more exuberantly imaginative, have descried in these two passages fragments of what was once a whole epic poem on the history of ancient Israel from the Conquest of Canaan to David's assumption of the kingship. The term *Hayyāshār*, "the Upright," of the title is most often held to refer either to heroes celebrated in the various poems of the "anthology," or to Israel as the upright nation; in the latter case, a relationship has been seen between "Jashar," (= *Hayyāshār*), and "Jeshurun," the poetic name of Israel found at Deut. 32:15, 33:5 and 33:26 and Isa. 44:2.

This view of the exclusively poetic or even epic character of SH rests upon the assumption that the book included both the poetry cited in Josh. 10:12-13 and that of David's lament. Now there is no doubt that the verse of the Joshua passage was at one time contained in SH: the "that" of the words "Is not that written in *The Book of the Upright*" can only refer to the several immediately preceding poetic lines. But no such explicit ascription of David's lament to SH is stated in II Sam.

---

[27] So far as I am able to ascertain, this conception of the nature and contents of SH has hitherto been contradicted by no major modern discussion of, or commentary on, the two crucial passages.

1:17-18, the prose introduction to the poetry of the lament.
The notion that *The Book of the Upright* ever included David's
elegy is just an inference from the mistaken interpretation
given II Sam. 1:18, the latter part of the introductory statement in prose. What in fact is stated in this passage is that
the injunction to teach Israel *qsht* (discussed below) "is,
indeed, written in the Book of the Upright." *The injunction to
teach qsht*, that is, *not the poetic verses of David's lament*, is what
*The Book of the Upright* contained.

   If this construction of II Sam. 1:18 is correct, be it noted,
if David's lament over Saul and Jonathan was never a part
of SH, then this book was something other than the anthology of poems about ancient Israelite heroes that it has hitherto been held to be. What that "something other" was must
take the Joshua passage into account; what SH was not—
namely a book of exclusively poetic or epic character—
emerges from the following demonstration that it was not
David's elegiac poetry that II Sam. 1:18 ascribes to *The Book
of the Upright*, but an injunction stated in prose.

   The Hebrew word *qsht*—*qesheth* ("bow") as vocalized by
the Massoretes—is plainly the crux of the difficulty of II Sam.
1:18. As between the two main textual assumptions involved
in the various attempts, ancient and modern, to interpret the
verse—that this Hebrew word was always part of the text,
or that the word was not originally there[28]—the text-critical
rule requiring retention of the more difficult reading entails
rejection of the latter assumption: that the word was always
in the text is clearly far more probable than that it was not.

   In the belief that the difficult *qsht* must be retained, there
have been various attempts to explain it, or to emend it. The
simplest and therefore the best of these attempts is the
suggestion, advanced by more than one scholar during the
past hundred years, to read the word *qāshōth* "hard things,
harsh things. difficulties," rather than *qāsheth* (pausal form of

---

[28] Following the procedure of one important manuscript of the Septuagint (Codex B), many translators and commentators simply omit the difficult *qsht* of the Hebrew text. This results in an awkward rendering of v.
18, to the effect that David ordered his elegy—declared already "written
in the Book of Jashar"—to be taught to the people of Judah.

*qesheth*) "bow."[29] This involves a change only in the Massoretic
vowel-points, not in the consonants of the much earlier, originally unvocalized text. The suggestion to read *qāshōth* for
*qāsheth* would quite probably long since have won its way
into general acceptance, had the rest of verse 18 been given
satisfactory interpretation. But the emergence of such an
interpretation was blocked by the misguided attempt to read
into the rest of verse 18 an ascription of the entire lament to
*The Book of the Upright.*

Incorporating the suggestion to read *qāshōth* rather than
*qāsheth*, we obtain the following quite literal translation of II
Samuel 1:17-19:

> [17]And David lamented with this lamentation over Saul
> and over Jonathan his son, [18]and then said, "'To teach the
> children of Judah hard things,' behold, is written in *The
> Book of the Upright.*"

> [19]"The Beauty, O Israel, is slain," etc.

Rather more freely translated, the passage reads:

> [17]When David had made the following lamentation over
> Saul and over Jonathan his son, [18]he said, "'To teach the
> Judeans harsh facts' is, indeed, written in *The Book of the
> Upright.*"

> [19]"The Beauty," etc.

Verses 17 and 18 are thus a tersely-worded introduction
to David's poetic lamentation, in which David is quoted as
justifying his dirge's potentially baneful, public admission of
Israel's defeat by holding its utterance authorized—or rather
necessitated—by the written injunction of *The Book of the Upright.*[30]
There is nothing in the passage, so understood, of any order
by David that the Judeans be taught this particular dirge; nor

---

[29] S. R. Driver, *Notes on the Hebrew Text and the Topography of the Books of Samuel*, 2nd ed. (Oxford, 1913), 234; G. A. Smith, *The Early Poetry of Israel in its Physical and Social Origins* (London, 1912), 96-97.

[30] Note the presumption: *words* ominous of ill for oneself and one's people are normally to be avoided. But for this divine instruction, forma-tive of part of Judah's way in the world and so recorded in SH, David's elegy might not have been publicly voiced at all.

is it stated that the dirge was written in *The Book of the Upright*; nor does the writer of this section of Samuel claim exclusively for his own the reference to *The Book of the Upright*, but rather puts it in David's mouth—a fact of some importance, as we shall see. All the misconceptions just mentioned, however, are present in our most commonly accepted translations and commentaries, which thus reflect and lend currency to the mistaken but now prevailing view of the nature and contents of SH.

On the showing of our Samuel passage, it can not successfully be argued either that David's poetic lament ever constituted part of *The Book of the Upright*, or that the *Book* was exclusively poetic or epic in character.

II

We have thus far shown what SH was not: it was certainly no collection of heroic poetry. Actually, our demonstration has taken us a little beyond this negative conclusion. We have seen that *The Book of the Upright* was the sort of book that could contain an injunction respecting the Judeans, an order presumably addressed to those in a position to carry it out; it was an injunction, moreover, so authoritative that a leader like the future King of Israel, David, could appeal to it in justification of an act of his that might otherwise have been censurable. Is this hint as to the nature and contents of *The Book of the Upright* borne out, or contradicted, by the evidence of the other passage, Josh. 10:12-14, in the course of which our *Book* was mentioned by name?

It will be remembered that there is no doubting the fact that the poetic lines of verses 12-13 of this passage once stood in *The Book of the Upright*; so that the combined evidence of both scriptural passages suggests that our *Book*, while not exclusively devoted to heroic poetry, did contain both poetry of the sort found in the Joshua 10 citation and such a prose injunction as that of II Sam. 1:18. It must also be observed, however, that the Joshua passage attributed somewhat more to *The Book of the Upright* than the lines of poetry directly quoted, and this additional material, while in our passage it is indirectly cited—or rather paraphrased—must at least have commenced in prose. Thus, if the citation of SH in II Samuel was clearly a prose injunction, that of Joshua 10, as it originally stood in SH, consisted of prose-plus-poetry, a prose context that included the poetic context drawn from the original *The Book of the Upright*, judging by what is left of it in Josh. 10-12, was of an injunctive character; and it is this injunctive character, the point in common between the citations of *The Book of the Upright* both here in Joshua and in II Samuel, which must be taken into account in trying to determine the original nature and function of *The Book of the Upright*.

Unfortunately, the text of this passage in Joshua, as stated earlier, has not been accurately translated and understood, with the result that some important aspects of the citation of *The Book of the Upright*, and other information about the *Book* contained in the passage, have remained obscure or been distorted. A translation and interpretation of the passage which will allow its data about SH to be more clearly seen must now, therefore, be proposed.

Joshua 10, we may recall, begins with an account of how Joshua and the Israelite army, in a forced march from Gilgal, came to the relief of their Gibeonite allies who had been attacked by the combined forces of five kings of the Amorites. The Amorites, defeated at Gibeon, were pursued by the men of Israel; as the Amorites in their flight were on the declivity between Upper Beth Horon and Lower Beth Horon, near the point where the Valley of Ayalon debouches westward, the Lord hurled great hailstones down upon them, so that, the narrator tells us in verse 11, "more were done to death by the hailstones than the Israelites slew by the sword." At this point in the chapter, verse 12, our passage begins and continues through verses 13 and 14. Although verse 13 contains an instance of faulty word-division (see below), the consonantal text is otherwise perfectly preserved.

Following are a translation and a brief exposition of the main points of difference between my corrected reading of the passage and the chief commonly accepted interpretations:

¹²This was when Joshua made his speech to the Lord: "On the day of the Lord's setting the Amorites before the men of Israel, He said, as Israel looked on,

> 'Sun, representing Gibeon, stand still,
> and Moon, representing the Valley of Ayalon!'
> ¹³And the sun stood still,
> and the moon paused,
>> the witnesses of the stand of the
>> people of His foes.

Is not that written in *The Book of the Upright*?" Thereupon the sun paused in the midst of the heavens, not hasting to set for about a whole day. ¹⁴Neither before nor since has there been the like of that day for the Lord's heeding a man's voice; because it was the Lord who fought for Israel.

¹²*This was when* ...—The usual rendering of *'āz* = "Then" (in the sense of time subsequent to that of the previous narrative) is awkward here because if, as we are told in verse 11, the Amorites had already been routed and slain, why need Joshua have "then" addressed the Lord? The solution to the difficulty emerges from the observation that in Biblical Hebrew usage the particle *'āz*, followed as it is here by the imperfect verb-form in a *past* context, is not temporally consequential, but rather refers and temporarily links the sequel to the *context as a whole*; and the imperfect verb-form expresses an action thought of as taking place *prior* to the actions described as completed in the preceding portion of the text. "This was when ..." here means that Joshua's address is to be thought of as taking place at a time in advance of—though in the narrative as set down it succeeds—the previously described smiting of the Amorites by the Lord's lethal hailstones. The usage, as was pointed out above,[31] is an efficient rhetorical and redactional means of introducing additional material, or material from an extraneous source, while not disrupting the sequence of an immediately preceding bloc of narration.

*Joshua made his speech to the Lord:* —Joshua's speech is *to the Lord*, not *with the Lord*. "With the Lord"[32] reflects the attempt of many interpreters to deal with the awkwardness

---

[31] Chapter Four, §1 and n. 25.

[32] See, e.g., the translation in the New English Bible.

resulting from their mistaken belief that, although Joshua is stated to have spoken to the Lord, he "really" spoke to the sun and the moon. The text of the verse states, however, that Joshua addressed a speech *to the Lord* in which he declared that the *Lord*, on a particular day, had addressed commands to the sun and the moon.

   *"On the day of the Lord's setting the Amorites before the men of Israel..."* —These—not, as in most modern versions, the vocative addressing of the sun and the moon—are the opening words of Joshua's speech to the Lord. The "day" mentioned by Joshua here is not, as usually understood, the day of Joshua's speech and of the Amorites' defeat, but some previous day on which Israel's attack upon the Amorites had been foreshadowed. "Setting ... before" here, as frequently, means "putting ... at the disposal of";[33] on the day referred to, that is, the Lord had apparently commanded Israel to attack the Amorites and had indicated that Israel's attack would be successful: the Lord would deliver the Amorites into Israel's hand (cf. verse 8). As it once stood in SH, accordingly, the prose context of the ensuing lines of poetry, judging by the reflection of it in these opening words of Joshua's speech, must have been devoted to an account of how the Lord commanded Israel to attack the Amorites; it was, that is to say, a *prose passage essentially and notably injunctive in character.* Joshua, it ought perhaps to be remarked, addresses the Lord in the third person, as superiors are addressed in Biblical Hebrew.

   *"... He said, as Israel looked on, 'Sun ... and Moon ...'"* —Not Joshua, but the Lord, is thus declared (in words put in Joshua's mouth) to have apostrophized the sun and moon. If "Joshua" and not "the Lord" were the antecedent of the "He" of "He said," Biblical Hebrew usage would here require specific reference to Joshua by name. The generally accepted assumption that the text attributes to Joshua, rather than to the Lord, the issuance of commands to the sun and

---

[33] Cf. the usage at Deut. 1:21, 2:36, 7:2 and 23, 31:5, Judg. 11:9, I Kings 9:6, etc.

moon—an assumption that goes back to the Septuagint—
thus rests upon a violation of Biblical Hebrew syntax.[34]

*"Sun, representing Gibeon, stand still, and Moon, represent-
ing the Valley of Ayalon!"* —The usual renderings, which
make the sun and moon halt *in* or *at* Gibeon and the Valley
of Ayalon respectively, can scarcely be correct. The underlying Hebrew preposition ($b^e$-) was not, apparently, used in
Biblical Hebrew to express presence of the sun and moon, as
physical bodies "in" or "at" any save some heavenly locale.
We have here an instance of the use of this preposition to
introduce a secondary predicate: "Sun *as* [or: representing]
Gibeon ... Moon *as* the Valley of Ayalon."[35]

We must, I think, understand the commands addressed
by the Lord to the sun and moon as made by Him in the
course of the proposal to attack the Amorites to which Joshua
has alluded in the opening words of his speech. "As Israel
looked on," the Lord gave them a "sign" that had both
geographical and temporal significance. In terms of geogra-
phy, the "sign" meant that Israel's victory over the Amorites
would be won in an area whose eastern and western limits
respectively were marked by Gibeon and the Valley of
Ayalon, the places "represented" by the sun and the moon.
In terms of time, the "sign" indicated that the battle would
continue until moon-rise, indeed, but not after sun-set, so
that both heavenly bodies would "witness" the last of the
Amorite "stand."

---

[34] The false assumption was not, however, shared by Ben Sira (*ca.* 189
B.C.E.) who, in the section of his "Let us now praise famous men" devoted
to Joshua the son of Nun wrote:

"Was not the sun held back by his hand?
    And did not one day become as long as two?
He called upon the Most High, the Mighty One,
    When enemies pressed him on every side,
and the Great Lord answered him
    with hailstones of mighty powers" (Ecclesiasticus 46:4-6a).

Note, too, that Ben Sira takes the same view of *'āz* followed by an imperfect verb-form as that pointed out above; he regarded Joshua's address to
the Lord as having taken place *before* the Lord's answer, the smiting of the
Amorites "with hailstones of mighty power."

[35] F. Brown, S.R. Driver, C. A. Briggs, *A Hebrew and English Lexicon of the
Old Testament* (Oxford, 1955), 88-89 §I, 7b; the so-called *beth essentiae*.

13a*"And the sun stood still and the moon paused ..."* —The heavenly bodies' obedient performance of the "sign," as commanded by the Lord, is thus reported. This *earlier* stoppage of the sun and moon, in contrast to that of the sun mentioned in 13b, was presumably of short duration, since it need have lasted only long enough to constitute the "sign" for onlooking Israel.[36]

*"... the witnesses of the stand of the people of His foes."* —This phrase, in appositional parallelism to "sun" and "moon," ends the stanza of poetry directly quoted from SH by Joshua in the course of his speech to the Lord. My translation, while involving no alternation of any consonant of the Hebrew text, assumes that the word-division of the consonants here is slightly different from that of our traditionally transmitted text. The latter— *'adh-yiqqōm goy ōyᵉbhāw*—is generally given some such rendering as "until (*'adh*) the nation (*goy*) took vengeance on (*yiqqōm*) its enemies (*ōyᵉbhāw*)." So to translate, however, violates Hebrew usage. "To take vengeance upon" requires the verb *nāqam* (the root of the form *yiqqōm*) to be connected with its object by means of either the preposition *min* or *lᵉ-*. Indeed, unless the Hebrew text be emended to include one or other of these prepositions, the only grammatically correct translation of the phrase as vocalized in our Massoretic text would be the plainly nonsensical "... until a people should *avenge* its foes" —i.e., not "wreak vengeance *upon*," but "take revenge *for* its foes," the very opposite of the sense as generally rendered.[37]

The difficulty vanishes once it is realized that the consonants of our received text, instead of being divided so as to read *'d yqm gwy'byw*, ought rather to have been divided so as to read *'dy qm gwy'byw*. By this simple back-spacing of a single consonant (*yōdh*), we exchange the nonsensical "until (*'adh*) a people should avenge its foes" for the contextually apt "... the witness of (*'ēdhē*) the stand of (*qūm*) the people of His foes." Faulty word-division owing to transplacement of

---

[36] Cf. the expressly mentioned use of the sun to constitute the "sign" to Hezekiah in Isa. 38:7-8; II Kings 20:8-11.

[37] See Brown-Driver-Briggs, *Lexicon* (n. 32, above), 667-668.

a single letter from the end of one word to the beginning of the next is quite common in the Hebrew Bible.[38]

According to the "sign" as given and as written down in *The Book of the Upright*, Joshua reminds the Lord, the battle with the Amorites was not only to take place in the area bounded by Gibeon and the Valley of Ayalon, represented by the sun and moon respectively, but these bodies were to be "the witnesses of" ( $'dy = 'ēdhē$ ) the "stand" ( $qm = qūm$ ) to be put up by the people of God's foes. That is to say, the moon was to have risen before the Amorites were crushed, but the sun was not to have set. At the moment of Joshua's speech, however, the Amorite "stand" was still apparently far from in its final phase, and it was already midday. What, then, of the Lord's promise, given in his sign?

*"Is not that written in The Book of the Upright?"* —Joshua's speech to the Lord is concluded with this rhetorical question. The word "that" here embraces both the foreshadowing of the attack upon the Amorites and the "sign" guaranteeing victory. Accordingly, *The Book of the Upright*, as referred to by Joshua, contained an instruction to Israel, which Israel had obeyed, and a divine promise to Israel—a promise which, Joshua delicately suggests, it may soon be too late to properly fulfill. The *Book* is appealed to by Joshua as attesting both the now-heeded instruction and the as yet unfulfilled, though word-introduced and "sign"-guaranteed, promise.

[13b]*Thereupon the sun paused in the midst of the heavens, not hastening to set for about a whole day.* —The Lord's response to Joshua's speech, the hurling down of the lethal hailstones upon the Amorites, has already been given by the narrator in verse 11. Here he reports the remarkable concomitant effect of the speech: the prevention of the sun from setting so that, in literal fulfillment of the "sign," it, as well as the moon, might be a "witness" of the relatively brief duration of the Amorite stand against Israel. The moon is not mentioned, since the fighting was not in any case expected to be over before the usual appearance of the moon, which could thus act as "witness" without further divine interven-

---

[38] A considerable number of such instances is listed in F. Delitzsch, *Die Lese- und Schreibfehler im Alten Testament* (Berlin/Leipzig, 1920), 3.

tion. What was in question was the sun, which—as Joshua hinted delicately in his speech—would certainly have normally set before the complete downing of the Amorites, hence would not have been able to fulfill its "sign"-designated function.

The pausing of the sun mentioned in this second half of verse 13 is usually understood as an amplified version of the same stoppage of both sun and moon reported in the first half of the verse.[39] In such case, however, 13b is strictly speaking superfluous; and even granting that the prolixity is tolerable in a context otherwise so tersely phrased, we should still be at a loss to account for the omission here of any mention of the moon. These difficulties disappear, of course, once it is realized that the stoppage of 13a derives from the account in *The Book of the Upright* quoted by Joshua in the course of his speech to the Lord, the stoppage that figured in the "sign" held to have been given by the Lord on the day when the attack on the Amorites was proposed; whereas the stoppage of 13b is the one that assertedly occurred in fulfillment of the "sign" on the later day of the battle itself.

[14]*Neither before nor since has there been the like of that day for the Lord's heeding a man's voice; because it was the Lord who fought for Israel.* —With this observation the narrator concludes his account of Joshua's intercession and of the Lord's response, a response that, according to him, most remarkably and exactly fulfilled the terms of the "sign" of victory the Lord gave Israel in bidding them attack the Amorites. His presentation of Joshua's intercessory speech to the Lord, we observe, consists of a partly paraphrased, partly quoted, citation of *The Book of the Upright*. The paraphrased portion of the citation is in prose, the directly quoted portion is in poetry. As the paraphrased portion narrates a divine proposal and injunction, the original in *The Book of the Upright* which it thus summarizes was doubtless in prose also. And the fact that the paraphrase of this portion of the citation from *The Book of the Upright*—in contradistinction to the directly-quoted following lines of poetry, though both are put in Joshua's

---

[39] See the various commentaries and translations.

mouth—is the work of the writer or compiler of this section of our Scriptural Book of Joshua suffices to demonstrate that our Scriptural author knew *The Book of the Upright* at first hand.

The differences between the currently accepted interpretation of Joshua 10:12-14 and that presented above are very considerable. In the latter, the passage is seen to be far more integrated in itself, and better articulated with what precedes it in the chapter, than in the regnant view. Moreover, a number of awkwardnesses disappear when the passage is given the interpretation provided here. First, the opening word, "Then," and "in/on the day of the Lord's setting the Amorite before the men of Israel," are shown to refer to two different days, and not the same day. Second, we avoid the inconsequence of introducing what is supposedly Joshua's directly quoted apostrophization of the sun and the moon with a statement declaring these words of Joshua's speech to the Lord; in fact, the passage has the Lord, not Joshua, apostrophizing the heavenly bodies, with Joshua, in his address to Him, pointing out that He has done this. Third, by making the citation of *The Book of the Upright* a part of Joshua's speech to the Lord, we avoid the awkwardness of supposing that the narrator has clumsily made this reference, and then said a second time part of what had just been given in the quotation from the *Book*; the difficulty of the apparently otiose repetition is resolved when it is seen that the sun-stoppage of the quotation is not the same as the sun stoppage of the ensuing narrative.

Naturally, and most importantly from the point of view of our main concern, the difficulties involved in the regnant understanding of the passage have obscured and distorted its evidence for the nature and functioning of SH. *The Book of the Upright* was plainly something quite different from the anthology of ancient poetry, or national epic, that it is commonly asserted to be.

### III

Let us now consider the facts about SH which the foregoing attempts to achieve more accurate understanding of our sources—the two key passages in Joshua and II Samuel—have disclosed.

1) Quite plainly, SH contained the Lord's directives—
   commands, injunctions, instructions, and the like—for the
   guidance and governance of Israel. Only less obviously,
   the *Book* also contained promises made by the Lord to
   Israel, accompanied by narration of whatever "sign" or
   "wonder" may have been manifested as warranty that a
   particular promise would be fulfilled. Both prose and
   poetry were employed in articulating this subject-matter.

2) The authoritative character of the *Book* is revealed in
   the variant purposes for which Joshua and David are
   represented as citing it. Joshua appeals to it in intercession with the Lord on Israel's behalf during the
   battle against the Amorites; in this case what is
   recorded in SH is patently believed to be binding on
   the Lord. David, on the other hand, appeals to it in
   defending his public lament over Saul and Jonathan
   with its dispiriting admission of defeat of God's
   people at the hands of the Philistines; his lament, he
   claims, is justified by a divine injunction recorded in *The
   Book of the Upright*—an injunction respecting his fellow-
   Judeans that is assumed to be especially binding upon
   such a leader as himself.

3) That two such leaders as Joshua and David are made
   the citers of *The Book of the Upright* implies a special
   relationship between the *Book* and Israel's leadership; we are also thus apprised that the *Book* is
   believed to have retained its importance and relevance for Israel's leadership (and for Israel) over a
   period of more than two hundred years.

4) In the citation attributed to David, it is the *Judeans*, rather
   than all Israelites, who by divine command are to be
   given instruction in "harsh facts." We are not told the
   reason for this particularity, but the fact of it seems to point
   to the inclusion, within SH, of divine responses in circumstances affecting a section, rather than the whole, of the
   people of Israel. And this implies a collection of such
   responses from more than one part of Israel throughout
   the two centuries or so between Joshua's day and David's.

So considered, *The Book of the Upright* was a corpus of
divine commandments, injunctions, instructions and propos-
als to Israel, or to constituent parts of Israel, as well as of
divine promises to Israel, which were written down and
added to the corpus as they were issued from time to time
throughout a period of somewhat more than two centuries.
Not less than the injunctions were held sacredly binding
upon Israel, and especially on Israel's leadership, the promises were deemed sacredly binding upon the Lord of Hosts.
It is in the character of the commandments and the promises
as sacredly obligatory upon the two parties respectively that
we must, I believe, seek the explanation of the word
"upright" in the book's title. The "upright" is the "right
thing," the thing that rightly ought to be done, whether by
Israel in obedience to God, or by God in fulfilling His promises to Israel. The sense of the word in our title is thus the
same as at Deut. 6:18, where we read "And you shall do what
is right and good in the sight of the Lord," and again at Deut.
32:4 where the Lord is declared "a God of faithfulness ... just
and right is He."

The author of the Aramaic paraphrase titled *Targum
Jonathan* had a very correct perception of the contents of *The
Book of the Upright* when he translated the Hebrew title,
*Sēpher Hayyāshār*, both at Josh. 10:13 and at II Sam. 1:18. as
*Siphrā dhe'ōrāyethā*, "the Book of the Torah."[40] For certainly
*The Book of the Upright* consisted of just such revelations of
the divine will to "men of God" and "servants of the Lord"
like Moses and Joshua, as our Scriptures call *tōrāh, tōrōth*.[41]
When, at Exod. 17:14, we read:

"And the Lord said to Moses, 'Write this as a record in
the book, and put it in Joshua's ears, that I shall assur-
edly blot out the remembrance of Amalek from under the
heavens,'"

it may well be that "the book" in question was none other

---

[40] *Miqrā'ōth Gedhōlōth: Nebhī'īm Rīshonīm* (New York, 1946), 20b; cf., too
the commentaries of Rashi and Kimchi on these passages.

[41] Brown-Driver-Briggs, *Lexicon*, 435a-436b, especially the passages
listed under 2.

than SH.[42] Like *The Book of the Upright* as cited in Joshua 10
and II Samuel 1, so the book of this passage in Exodus was
to function as testimony to the fact that this divine utterance
had been "issued" and must some day arise out of its word-
form to constitute part of the world's reality.

The genesis and development of the literature before us
in the Hebrew Bible owe far more than is commonly
acknowledged to this "testimonial" or "witnessing" function
of written words.[43] The compilers of the initial portion of our
Scriptures—the great work composed early in King
Solomon's reign—not only knew and drew upon *The Book of
the Upright*, but were plainly moved to compose their Scripture by motives not very much different from those that we
have seen to be operative in the earlier book. May it not be,
indeed, that much of the content of *The Book of the Upright* was
included in the Scripture as written down in Solomon's day?
And that it was because *The Book of the Upright* was thus superseded that it disappeared from view? Whatever the reason for the
disappearance of *The Book of the Upright*, we may certainly see
it as an immediate forerunner of the oldest section of our
Hebrew Bible, a work conceived and held to function in
terms of ancient Israel's perception of literature, a named
and identifiable stage in the process that ultimately resulted
in our Old Testament.

---

[42] So, too, "the book" of I Sam. 10:25. The argument, sometimes
advanced, that "in *the* book" here and elsewhere does not mean "in *the*
book already in use," but is rather the equivalent to "in *a* book," "on *a*
scroll," is not compelling. It is not borne out, if not contradicted, by the
usage of "on *a* book-scroll" at Deut. 17:18, 13:24, Josh. 18:9, and Jer. 45:1.

[43] See Chapter Two, §5, above.

# CHAPTER SIX

## THE HEBREW SCRIPTURES AS A LITERARY UNIT

Properly to understand the Hebrew Bible we must, I think, come to see that these Scriptures, although composed, edited and redacted over a time-span of many centuries, and diverse as their numerous texts undeniably are, were nevertheless brought together in order to constitute a literary unity, form a literary whole. The main groupings and the individual books of the Hebrew Bible cannot begin to be correctly interpreted if the entire corpus is not grasped and taken into account.

The literary unity of the Hebrew Bible, it should be emphasized, is not that of an archive, of a library, of an encyclopedia, or of an anthology. As originally constituted it was not yet even the unity of a "canon" of Holy Scripture, such as later Jews and early Christians were variantly to see in it. The literary unity we are here seeking to describe is rather that of a body of writings, deliberately brought together in order to achieve a certain purpose, an integrated grouping of texts whose creation and transmission proceeded entirely in terms of ancient Israel's assumptions about the nature and function of literature. The central purpose and the precanonical unity of the Hebrew Scriptures can, accordingly, not be apprehended apart from the perception of literature that was culturally operative in ancient Israel: the postulates and conventionally held and transmitted beliefs studied in the several preceding chapters. Two of those beliefs, as we shall see, are especially important in this regard.

Before proceeding with our attempt to apprehend and to state the unity of the Hebrew Scriptures, let us remind ourselves that those Scriptures, as we now have them, comprise three great divisions. The first of these is "Torah," the Pentateuch or Five Books of Moses. The second is "Prophets," subdivided into "Former Prophets" and "Latter Prophets"; the Former Prophets include the books of Joshua, Judges, Samuel and Kings, while the Latter Prophets consist of four collections of written prophecy: Isaiah, Jeremiah, Ezekiel, and the Twelve so-called "minor" (meaning "shorter") prophets. And the third great division is called the "Writings," or "Hagiography": this includes Psalms, Proverbs, Job, Song of Songs, Ruth, Lamentations, Ecclesiastes, Esther, Daniel, Ezra and Chronicles. This last division, as shown by the Septuagint, the pre-Christian Greek version of the Hebrew Bible, at one time almost certainly included other books than those just mentioned; some of these, canonized by the Early Church, were included in its "Old Testament"; still later, by Protestants, they were again separated out and circulated as "Apocrypha." Be this as it may, the pre-canonical Hebrew Scriptures were already regarded as assembled in a tri-partite division that has maintained itself down to the present day. Indeed, the commonest modern Jewish designation of the tri-divisional Scriptures is an acronym, T⁰nakh, made up of the initial letters of the Hebrew words for each respective division: "T" for Tōrāh (often, somewhat misleadingly, translated "Law"), "N" for N⁰bhī'īm ("Prophets"), and "K" for K⁰thūbhīm ("Writings"). We have a second pre-Christian century attestation (ca. 130 B.C.E.) of what is generally considered this very tri-divisional grouping: in the Prologue to Ecclesiasticus, or the Wisdom of Jesus the Son of Sirach (a book included in the Apocrypha), mention is made of "the Law and the Prophets and the other Books of our fathers."[44] As already mentioned (Chapter Four, §1 above), the Jewish pietists who earlier in the second century B.C.E. produced the Qumran ("Dead Sea") Scrolls must be credited with the invention of the earliest name known to us for the entire collected corpus of sacred literature: what we term "the

---

[44] The possibility has not been reckoned with, so far as I am aware, that this statement should be read: "... the Law-and-the-Prophets and the other Books of our fathers." In such case, the author of the Prologue, Ben Sira's grandson, would have held the same view of the bi-partite division of the Scriptures as is outlined below.

Bible" (from the Greek *ta biblia*, "the books"), they called "the Book(s) of Meditation" or "the Book(s) of Study."

It should not escape our notice that whereas we have specific names for the first two divisions of the assembled Scriptures, *Tōrāh* and *Nᵉbhī'īm* ("Law" and "Prophets"), we have a vague, catch-all designation for the third—*Kᵉthūbhīm* ("Writings"). The inventors and subsequent users of these divisional names thus recognized and expressed a contrast between the first two divisions on the one hand, and the third division on the other; the first two divisions were felt to be distinctive in a way in which the third division was not. There is another significant fact: ancient allusions to the divisions of the Hebrew Scriptures, such as those in the Apocrypha and in the New Testament, often speak of "the Law and the Prophets" together with no mention of the third division, or else specifically contrast "the Law and the Prophets" on the one hand with "the Writings" on the other; the Psalms, interestingly enough, can either be classed with "the Law and the Prophets," or subsumed among "the Writings." II Maccabees 15:9, for example, relates that Judas Maccabeus encouraged his men "from the Law and the Prophets"; IV Maccabees 18:10-18, first mentioning the "Law and the Prophets," proceeds with details cited not only from the Pentateuch and from the Prophets Isaiah and Ezekiel, but from such "Writings" as Daniel, Psalms and Proverbs. In the New Testament, the "Law and the Prophets" are nearly always cited without mention of the "Writings" (Matthew 5:7, 7:12, 11:13, 22:40; Luke 16:16; John 1:45; Acts 13:15, 24:14, 28:23; Romans 3:21); but in one passage, Luke 24:44, Jesus is quoted as saying that all that was written of him "in the Law of Moses and the Prophets and Psalms" had to be fulfilled; in this passage, then, the Psalms are classed with "Prophets."

These considerations point to an earlier *two-fold sectioning of the contents of the Scriptures*. The Scriptures, that is to say, so far as their subject-matter is concerned, were thought of by those who first assembled and transmitted them, as a *two-fold unity*. That they so thought is a natural consequence of ancient Israelite convictions about the nature and functioning of literature and of the assumptions embodied in those convictions.

Two of the ancient Israelite assumptions about words that were treated above—namely, that words can create reality, and that, in and of themselves, they can perform the function of a living witness—are the premises of the beliefs about the nature and functioning of literature that, to its creators and assemblers, made a literary unity of what we today call the T*enakh*, or Old Testament. Words can create: God's words especially, as perceived by ancient Israel's prophets, priests and sages, were the inner structure and quintessence of the world's reality, indeed the first adumbration or materialization of that reality. Words witness: God's words, written down, record and attest what is, or must come to be, really the case;[45] men's words, written down, record and attest the freely accepted obligations that are theirs to enact and fulfill. Words create: a human being, in desperate anxiety, fear, need or desire, can fashion a *māshāl*, a word-likeness, of the reality he would like to see actualized, and—God willing—this will function as a prefiguration, or presage, of what will come to be the case; there are, of course, many forms and kinds of such word-likenesses. Words witness: they attest both what must be accepted, acknowledged, lived by, if the entire divine-human-natural order is to endure, and the fact that such acceptance, acknowledgment, and life-intention has become part of the "soul" and social structure of the persons concerned. The ancient Israelite beliefs about the nature and functioning of literature that have been engendered by these two assumptions about words—the literary medium —are, accordingly, these:

(1) that literature is an articulating and structuring of words intended to constitute or prefigure actualities of the "real world"; and

---

[45] Hence the *pesher*-texts of the Dead Sea Scrolls, mistakenly called "commentaries," such as those to Habakkuk, Isaiah, Nahum and Psalm 37. These texts consist of *presagings* of the "holy words" in the scriptural books concerned—the indications of the "realities," whether of the past, the present (of the presager), or of the future, held to be laid up in those words, and thus either already fulfilled, in course of fulfillment, or awaiting future fulfillment. Cf. W. H. Brownlee, *The Midrash Pesher of Habakkuk* (Missoula, 1979), 26-28, and the present writer's review of this volume in *Journal of the American Oriental Society* CII (1982), 191-192.

(2) that literature is composed of various word-struc-
tures whereby, and wherein, the actualities of the
"real world," past, present, and future, and the implications of those actualities for those persons whom
they concern, are attested and acknowledged.

Proceeding by the light of these ancient Israelite assumptions and convictions, we are able quite readily to apprehend
the unity and central purpose of the collected Hebrew Scriptures. Before us in those Scriptures is the *word-form*, as the
producers and assemblers believed, of the world's reality,
the great system comprised of God, man and nature: the
word-form of the divinely-intended functioning of that
system, the testimonies to the effect that the system is indeed
the will of God, and the additional attestations of human
acceptance of the system and of faith in its coming ultimately
into complete actualization as intended and "worded" by God.

There is no part of the Hebrew Scriptures that is not, in
one way or another, connected with the creation and setting-
in of this great scheme: it is the tremendous concept of this
system that relates and links together and gives unity to the
many disparate texts and diverse books of the Hebrew Bible.
And the overriding purpose of assembling these writings
into a united whole was so that they might constitute the
attested word-form of the divine plan, a thus-concentrated
essence of the world's reality and reality-to-be. Here, in
word-essence, was God's creation of every part of the world-
system; and here, too, was not only attestation that the
system was indeed the intention of God, but attestation as
well of the necessary willingness of the representative
human agents of the system—Israel—to assume their role in
the functioning of the system. The unity of the assembled
Hebrew Scriptures is, in consequence of ancient Israel's
perception of the nature and functioning of literature, the
unity of a creative intention, already thus enacted in word-
essence, and destined to be fully actualized: the creative
intention of God.

Prophet-mediated "Torah" and "Attestation" are, accordingly, the two reciprocal and interconnected kinds of material of which the unified and assembled Hebrew Scriptures

are composed. Reference is made to just such a bi-partite unity in the 8th chapter of Isaiah ("First Isaiah"), a passage which can hardly be later than the end of the 8th century B.C.E. "Bind up Attestation," says Isaiah in verse 16, "seal Torah among my disciples." The cognate word to Isaiah's term *tᵉ῾ûdhāh* "attestation," the word usually translated "testimony" (*῾ēdhûth*), often occurs in the sense of "witnessing-words"; thus, "the testimony" of Exod. 25:16 means the words written on "the tables of stone" (Exod. 24:12); at Deut. 4:44-45 we read of the "testimonies, the statutes and the ordinances, which Moses spoke to the children of Israel when they came out of Egypt"; and there are many other examples.

According to the prophet Isaiah, then, the two-fold content of the divine revelation in written form, as he knew it, consisted of "Torah"—the creating, instituting, commanding words which were so many emanations of the divine will, the words constitutive of reality, actual and yet-to-be—and of "Attestation"—the "witnessing-words" and the statement of human response. Notice that Isaiah pairs the terms "Torah" and "Attestation" in "synonymous parallelism"; "Torah" and "Attestation" could be used practically as synonyms because, obviously, each included and implied the other. There is reason to believe that the *Torah-and-Attestation* of Isaiah's reference was the great document—probably compiled from such earlier available texts as *The Book of the Upright* and other sources, and written down early in King Solomon's reign—which first brought together the attested word-form of the divine-human-natural system, a document still before us, by and large, in the Bible from Genesis to approximately I Kings 9. It is probable, too, that Isaiah's conception of Scripture as a two-fold unity was influential in the later assemblage of the supplemented and amplified Hebrew Bible.

By far the more important portion of the first of the two groupings of material which together comprise the unified collection of the Hebrew Scriptures—the grouping called "the Law (Torah) and the Prophets"—is made up of utterances attributed directly or indirectly to God. These utterances, as already remarked, were held to have created the

entire divine-human-natural order, with man set between
God and nature. Divine utterances, moreover, given mainly
through the prophet Moses, created the apparatus of link-
ages between God on the one hand, and man and the
phenomena of nature on the other, through which the entire
world-system was to be maintained and kept in good working order. The system was thought of as operating by virtue
of the divine power, or "holiness" (*qōdhesh*); and the apparatus created by divine utterances was designed to transmit
"holiness," God's power, in sufficient degree to all the rest
of His creation to sustain that creation and enable it successfully to function.

Now this apparatus was to be operated by a special
section of mankind, brought into being to perform this function, a people that was to constitute the link between God
and all the other nations that comprise mankind, and that,
through properly conditioned performance of the various
rites of the religious cults, was to mediate the sustaining
divine power to all natural phenomena, and thus assure the
continuing felicity of all peoples: through their progeny, the
three ancestral patriarchs of the "link-people" are promised,
all the nations of earth would receive blessing (Gen. 12:3,
18:18, 22:18, 26:4, 28:14). Israel, the "link-people," while it is
a part of mankind, is, like every other part of the holiness-
mediating apparatus, the special creation-by-word ("commandments," and the like) of God. The greater part of the Torah
and Former Prophets is concerned with the creation of Israel,
with the creation of the holiness-mediating apparatus, and
with the readying and discipling of Israel for its role in the
divine scheme of things. The Latter Prophets, again, are
collections of divine utterances concerned not alone with
Israel, but also with the other nations, particularly with those
nations whose impact and influence upon Israel were greatest; here too we find the oracles relating to, and constitutive
of, the ultimate setting in of the Great Scheme of God—the
eschatological prophets.

There are "witness"-words as well as divine "creating"-
words in the assembled Torah-and-Prophets. The historical
data and narratives which bulk so large in these portions of

Scripture are mainly attestations of the divine will regarding one or another component of the apparatus involved in this Great Scheme, most often, of course, regarding the "link-people," Israel. History, indeed, as we find it throughout the Hebrew Scriptures, is usually an attestation of a fulfillment of prophecy; and prophecy, we recall, is an introduction of a divine word into the world, a word constitutive of some reality. It is as attestedly-valid prophecy that history was held in ancient Israel to be of more than local or contemporary concern and interest. But though the "witness"-words in Torah-and-Prophets are present in quantity, they are, nevertheless, distinctly ancillary and subordinate to the reality-creating words of God; and the same subordination is true of the corollary "witness"-statement—expression of contrition and repentance for wrong-doing, professions of willingness to do God's will, refutations of rejectionist arguments, prayers for the setting-in of the fully operating Divine Scheme, and the like. In Torah-and-Prophets, the initiative is God's, the point of departure is with Him, and the material moves, as it were, from God toward man. "The Book of the Lord," indeed, is how at least part of Torah-and-Prophets is referred to at Isaiah 34:16—so called, no doubt, because the Lord is in very truth its protagonist.

In the Kethūbhīm—the Writings or Hagiography—on the other hand, emphasis is upon "witness" to the divine will, and upon the corollaries of such witness. Here the initiative is man's, especially as represented by Israel, and the movement of the material is directed from man toward God. The author-indicating first-person singular pronouns "I," "me," "my," "mine," so frequently encountered in the Psalter and in Lamentations, always signify Israel; the anonymous poets speak for and as the Israel they believed God intended Israel to become. Indeed, it is the Israel-God relationship, as seen from the vantage-point of Israel, that is the dominant theme of the Hagiography. This theme is carried out—this relationship is "witnessed"—in a multiple variety of forms and styles.

In fulfillment of prophecy, Israel's failure—possible in virtue of man's God-given endowment of freedom—to live as they had covenanted with the Lord resulted in exile and the destruction of their social and political structure. Recognition that they had brought these consequences upon themselves, their confession, repentance, prayers for forgiveness, and renewed expressions of intent to live by their covenant with the Lord—to fit themselves for, and to assume, the role assigned them in the Great Scheme of God—these are "witness"-motifs that recur most frequently in the Book of Lamentations and the Psalter. In Lamentations, bearing witness to the justice of her plight, Israel further attests readiness to assume her role in the Divine Plan, and prays for actualization of the prophesied Reign of God.

Poetic statements of all the Scriptural "witness"-themes are found in the Psalter; some of the so-called "wisdom"-psalms—e.g., Psalms 37 and 73—treat the problem posed by rejecters of God's plan and deniers of His justice. Especially characteristic of the Psalter is the previously mentioned (Chapter Three, §3) form of prayer that consists of stating as an accomplished fact what one ardently hopes and believes will one day be the case. Prime examples of these are the Psalms commencing "The Lord reigns"—Psalms 93, 97, 99—in which the Reign of God, the Divine Plan, is spoken of as though it had already come. It is in virtue of its handling of "witness"-themes that the Psalter was especially well-adapted to liturgical use in the Temple at Jerusalem, as well as in the public worship of the later Synagogue and the Church. At the same time, the Psalter's "witness" to God—and Israel's "I"-form expressions of faith, hope, trust and serene confidence in His saving power—have made the Psalter perhaps the finest book of private devotions available to suffering humanity in this world.

The Hagiography include three word-likenesses (*mashāls*) that attest aspects of the relationship between God and Israel. One of these consists of a group of ancient love-songs that have been reshaped and adapted into a figuration of the love of God for Israel and of Israel's love and longing for God: this is the Song of Songs. The Book of Ruth is a *mashāl* of the faithfulness that effects salvation. And the greatest of these *mashāls*, the Book of Job, attests Israel's faith that the Jobs of this world, whose doubt of the divine justice may be too deep and too well-founded to be eradicated by any human or man-mediated (prophetic) argument or reassurance, will ultimately be confronted and relieved of the agony of this doubt by God Himself.

Proverbs and Ecclesiastes are "wisdom-books," such as were used everywhere in the ancient Near East in the training of those necessary and influential functionaries and officials, the scribes. As the custodians and transmitters of the word-form of God's intention for the world—His Great Plan, that is—Israel's scribes were requited to be wholly convinced of, and deeply loyal to, the life-values and truth of that Plan: and these two books were designed to accomplish such conviction and loyalty. Proverbs, identifying Wisdom with God's intention, witnesses that only the scribe who lives by Wisdom so understood is truly successful as man and as official. Ecclesiastes is a defense of faith in the divine intention; it uses skepticism itself to negate that cynical skepticism of God's ultimate justice to which scribes in ancient Israel, as in every age, were only too prone.

Of the remaining Hagiography, Chronicles, with which belong the Books of Ezra and Nehemiah, is a history of the restoration of Israel from exile—hence a "witnessing" to the fulfillment of prophecy—in which Israel, with Davidically authorized provision for various aspects of the reinstituted Temple-worship, is depicted as ready to assume its role in the coming new world. The Book of David is a double *mashal*, or work of historical fiction: the purport is that the succession of world-empires, each of which has given way to the next as willed by God, must at length be superseded by God's own kingdom, which is to last forever. And the scroll of Esther, lastly, is a "witness"-*mashal* of God's providential care for Israel wherever Israel may be dispersed, so long as the people of Israel remain loyal to their covenant with God.

Thus, each of the two major components of the pre-canonical Hebrew Scriptures is by and large the complement of the other: the directed-at-man creation of a world-order based on love and justice, contained in Torah-and-Prophets, has in the Hagiography its schooled and disciplined, directed-to-God response of human acceptance. As expressed in the 85th Psalm,

Faithfulness springs up from earth,
and justice looks down from heaven.

From the point of view of the assemblers and compilers, the unity of the bi-partite Hebrew Scriptures was that of a cosmic dialogue: the "creating" words of God are answered by the "attesting" words of man.

In fine, the Hebrew Scriptures, to those who assembled them, were perceived as a great scheme of world order, created by God and freely accepted by man, as attested especially by Israel, the divinely instituted link-people between God and the families of mankind. Both the "creation" and the "attestation," by conventions and taken-for-granted assumption of ancient Israel's culture, were laid down in words. And as both were to last at least until the divine words had fully materialized as the world's reality, they were written down, and brought together into the Hebrew Bible as we have it. The Hebrew Scriptures are thus a literary unity: the written, attested word-form of the entire cosmic order as God was thought to have intended it to be and to function.

As first conceived, produced and transmitted, what came to be the T$^e$nakh of later Judaism, and the "Old Testament" of later Christianity, was culturally perceived by its creators and transmitters as the word-essence of the God-man-natural order, necessarily written down as literature. The conception of the Scriptures held in pre-Christian and pre-Talmudic Israel, although it is the source whence both the early Christian and the early "normative" Jewish conceptions of Holy Writ were derived, is not identical with either of these later conceptions. To early Christianity the Old Testament Scriptures were essentially a prefiguration of the Christ, and except as so considered would have no unifying principle, would be without focus and significance. To "normative" Judaism, again, the T$^e$nakh is an inexhaustible guide to the will of God for man, particularly for the people of Israel. But the earlier Israel which produced, assembled and transmitted the Scriptures as a bi-sectional literary unity, believed that those Scriptures were, as I have in this essay tried to show, the attested inmost matter, the essential structure, of the whole of the world's reality, as God, its creator, intended that reality to be and to function. As we read in the 14th chapter of Isaiah (verses 26-27):

> This is the plan prepared for the whole earth,
> this the hand stretched out over all the nations.
>> For the Lord of Hosts has prepared his plan:
>>> who shall frustrate it?
>> His is the hand stretched out,
>>> and who shall turn it back?

# BIBLIOGRAPHY

Albright, W. F. *Yahweh and the Gods of Canaan.* London, 1968.

Barr, J. *The Scope and Authority of the Bible.* Philadelphia, 1980.

Brown, F., S. R. Driver, and C. A. Briggs. *A Hebrew and English Lexicon of the Old Testament.* Oxford, 1955.

Brownlee, W. H. *The Midrash Pesher of Habakkuk.* Missoula, 1979.

*Cambridge History of the Bible* I. Cambridge, 1970.

Cassirer, E. *Language and Myth.* New York, 1946.

Cross, F. M., Jr. *The Ancient Library of Qumran and Modern Biblical Studies.* New York, 1958.

Delitzsch, F. *Die Lese- und Schreibfehler im Alten Testament.* Berlin/Leipzig, 1920.

Dürr, L. *Die Wertung des göttlichen Wortes im Alten Testament und in antiken Orient.* Leipzig, 1938.

Driver, S. R. *Notes on the Hebrew Test and the Topography of the Books of Samuel.* Oxford, 1913.

——————— *Introduction to the Literature of the Old Testament.* New York, 1914.

Eliot, T. S. "Religion and Literature." *Essays Ancient and Modern.* New York, 1936.

Elliott, R. C. *The Power of Satire: Magic, Ritual, Art.* Princeton, 1960.

Heimisch, P. *Das "Wort" im Alten Testament und in alten Orient.* Münster, 1923.

Izutsu, T. *Language and Magic.* Tokyo: Keio Institute of Philological Studies, 1965.

Jacobsen, T. *The Treasures of Darkness: A History of Mesopotamian Religion.* New Haven, 1976.

Levi, P. *The Drowned and the Saved*. New York, 1988.

Lewis, C. S. *The Literary Impact of the Authorized Version*. Philadelphia, 1967.

Lindblom, J. L. *Prophecy in Ancient Israel*. Oxford, 1962.

Malinowski, B. *Argonauts of the Western Pacific*. London, 1932.

Masing, H. *The Word of Yahweh*. Tartu, 1936.

May, H. G. and B. M. Metzger, eds. *The Oxford Annotated Bible ...*: *Revised Standard Version*. New York, 1973.

Rabinowitz, I. "The Qumran Authors' SPR HHGH/Y." *Journal of Near Eastern Studies* 20 (1961), 109-114.

————"Towards a Valid Theory of Biblical Hebrew Literature" in L. Wallach, ed., *The Classical Tradition: Literary and Historical Studies in Honor of Harry Caplan*. Ithaca, 1966, 315-328.

————"'Word' and Literature in Ancient Israel." *New Literary History*, IV (1972-1973), 119-139.

———— Review of W. H. Brownlee, *The Midrash Pesher of Habakkuk*. In *Journal of the American Oriental Society* CII (1982), 191-192.

————"ᶜAz Followed by Imperfect Verb-Form in Preterite Contexts: A Redactional Device in Biblical Hebrew." *Vetus Testamentum* 34 (1984), 53-62.

von Rad, G. *Old Testament Theology* II. Edinburgh, 1965.

Sandmel, S., ed. *The New English Bible ...* : *Oxford Study Edition*. New York, 1976.

Smith, G. A. *The Early Poetry of Israel in its Physical and Social Origins*. London, 1912.

Thiselton, A. C. "The Supposed Power of Words in the Biblical Writings." *Journal of Theological Studies* 25 (1974), 283-299.

Wellhausen, J. and H. H. Furness. *The Book of Psalms: A New English Translation*. New York, 1898.

Wiseman, D. J. "Books in the Ancient Near East and in the Old Testament." *The Cambridge History of the Bible* I. Cambridge, 1970.

# INDEX

# BIBLIOGRAPHY

## OF

# ISAAC RABINOWITZ*

I. BOOKS

1. "The Syriac Versions of Tobit." Unpublished Ph.D. Dissertation, Yale University, 1932.

2. Judah Messer Leon. *The Book of the Honeycomb's Flow/Sēpher Nōpheth Ṣūphīm. A Critical Edition and Translation.* Ithaca and London: Cornell University Press, 1983.

3. *A Witness Forever: Ancient Israel's Perception of Literature and the Resultant Hebrew Bible* edited with Afterwords by Ross Brann and David I. Owen (Occasional Publications of the Department of Near Eastern Studies and the Program of Jewish Studies Cornell University, Volume 1), Bethesda: CDL Press, 1993.

II. ARTICLES

1. "The Second and Third Columns of the Habakkuk Interpretation Scroll," *Journal of Biblical Literature* 69 (1950), 31-49.

2. "The Existence of a Hitherto Unknown Interpretation of Psalm 107," *Biblical Archaeologist* 14 (1951), 50-52.

3. "Trever's 'Taw' and Orlinsky's Argument," *Bulletin of the American Schools of Oriental Research* 124 (1951), 29.

4. "The Authorship, Audience and Date of the De Vaux Fragment of an Unknown Work," *Journal of Biblical Literature* 71 (1952), 19-32.

---

* We thank Mr. Joel Rabinowitz for his help with the compilation of his father's bibliography.

5. "Sequence and Dates of the Extra-Biblical Dead Sea Scroll-Texts and 'Damascus' Fragments," *Vetus Testamentum* 3 (1953), 175-185.

6. "A Hebrew Letter of the Second Century from Beth Mashko," *Bulletin of the American Schools of Oriental Research* 131 (1953), 21-24.

7. "A Reconsideration of 'Damascus' and '390 Years' in the 'Damascus' ('Zadokite') Fragments," *Journal of Biblical Literature* 73 (1954), 11-35.

8. "Aramaic Inscriptions of the Fifth Century B.C.E. from a North-Arab Shrine in Egypt," *Journal of Near Eastern Studies* 15 (1956), 1-9.

9. "The Guides of Righteousness," *Vetus Testamentum* 8 (1958), 391-404.

10. "Another Aramaic Record of the North-Arabian Goddess Han-'Ilat," *Journal of Near Eastern Studies* 18 (1959), 145-155.

11. "The Crux at Amos III 12," *Vetus Testamentum* 11 (1961), 228-231.

12. "The Qumran Authors' SPR HHGW/Y," *Journal of Near Eastern Studies* 20 (1961), 109-114.

13. "Government," In *Interpreters' Dictionary of the Bible* 2:E–J. Nashville, 1962, 451-462.

14. "'Be Opened' = ἐφφαθα (Mark 7 34): Did Jesus Speak Hebrew?" *Zeitschrift für die Neutestamentliche Wissenschaft* 53 (1962), 229-238.

15. "The Alleged Orphism of 11Q Pss 28:2-12 (=Psalm 151 LXX)," *Zeitschrift für die Neutestamentliche Wissenschaft* 76 (1964), 193-200.

16. "Towards a Valid Theory of Biblical Hebrew Literature," In L. Wallach, ed. *The Classical Tradition: Literary and Historical Studies in Honor of Harry Caplan*. Ithaca: Cornell University Press, 1966, 315-328.

17. "The Power of the Word: Memoranda for a Preface to the Scriptures," *Cornell Alumni News* 70/5 (1967), 12-16.

18. "The Meaning and Date of 'Damascus' Fragments, XI, 1,"
    *Revue de Qumran* 6 (1968), 433-435.

19. "Sephārad," In אנציקלופדיה מקראית ה [*Encyclopaedia Biblica* 5].
    (In Hebrew). Jerusalem, Israel, 1968, cols. 1100-1103.

20. "Paršegen/Patšegen," In ו אנציקלופדיה מקראית [*Encyclopaedia
    Biblica* 6]. (In Hebrew). Jerusalem, Israel, 1971, col. 625.

21. "Pat-Bāg," In ו אנציקלופדיה מקראית [*Encyclopaedia Biblica* 6]. (In
    Hebrew). Jerusalem, Israel, 1971, cols. 636-637.

22. "Pitgām/Pitgāmā," In ו אנציקלופדיה מקראית [*Encyclopaedia
    Biblica* 6]. (In Hebrew). Jerusalem, Israel, 1971, cols.
    637-638.

23. "ἔφφαθα (Mark vii.34): Certainly Hebrew, Not Aramaic,"
    *Journal of Semitic Studies* 16 (1971), 151-156.

24. "A Rectification of the Date of Judah Messer Leon's
    Death," In *Studies in Jewish Bibliography, History and
    Literature in Honor of I. Edward Kiev*. New York, 1971,
    399-406.

25. "The Qumran Original of Ben Sira's Concluding Acrostic
    on Wisdom," *Hebrew Union College Annual* 42 (1971),
    173-184.

26. "'Word' and Literature in Ancient Israel," *New Literary His-
    tory* 4 (1972-73), 119-139.

27. "'*Pēsher/Pittārōn*' Its Biblical Meaning and its Significance
    in the Qumran Literature," *Revue de Qumran* 8 (1973),
    219-232.

28. "Qeśîṭāh," In ז אנציקלופדיה מקראית [*Encyclopaedia Biblica* 7]. (In
    Hebrew). Jerusalem, Israel, 1976, col. 282.

29. "The Meaning of the Key ('Demetrius') Passage of the
    Qumran Nahum-Pesher," *Journal of the American Orien-
    tal Society* 98 (1978), 394-399.

30. "Sarah's Wish (Gen. XXI 6-7)," *Vetus Testamentum* 29
    (1979), 362-363.

31. "'*Az* Followed by Imperfect Verb-Form in Preterite Con-
    texts: A Redactional Device in Biblical Hebrew," *Vetus
    Testamentum* 34 (1984), 53-62.

32. "Pre-Modern Jewish Study of Rhetoric: An Introductory Bibliography," Rhetorica 3 (1985), 137-144.

33. "The Sardis Hebrew Inscriptions," In A. Seager, ed. *The Synagogue of Sardis and Its Setting (Archaeological Exploration of Sardis)*. Cambridge: Harvard University Press, forthcoming.

III. REVIEWS

1. Review of *Plato Arabus*, Volume II, *Alfarabius, De Platonis Philosophia*, by F. Rosenthal and R. Walzer. *American Journal of Philology* 67 (1946), 76-79.

2. Review of *Galen, on Medical Experience* (Arabic Version) by R. Walzer. *American Journal of Philology* 70 (1949), 437-440.

3. Review of *The Birth of the Bible: A New Approach*, by I. Lewy. *Jewish Social Studies* 13 (1951), 354-355.

4. Review of *Les manuscrits de la Mer Morte: Essai sur le Midrash d'Habacuc*, by M. Delcor. *Journal of Biblical Literature* 72 (1953), 136-137.

5. Review of *The Dead Sea Scrolls of St. Mark's Monastery*, Vols. I and II (Fascicle 2), by M. Burrows, *et al.*; *The Dead Sea Manual of Discipline: A Preliminary Survey*, by A. Dupont-Sommer; and *The Zadokite Fragments: Facsimile of the MSS*, by S. Zeitlin. *Jewish Social Studies* 15 (1953), 304-309.

6. Review of *The Zadokite Fragments and the Dead Sea Scrolls*, by H.H. Rowley. *Journal of Biblical Literature* 73 (1954), 253-255.

7. Review of *Papers of the Institute of Jewish Studies of University College, London*, Volume I, ed. by J. G. Weiss. *Journal of Semitic Studies* 14 (1969), 141-143.

8. Review of *Les Sadducéens*, by J. Le Moyne. *Revue de Qumran* 8 (1973), 271-276.

9. Review of *The Midrash Pesher of Habakkuk*, by W.H. Brownlee. *Journal of the American Oriental Society* 102 (1982), 191-192.

10. Review of *The Function and Use of the Imperfect Forms with Nun Paragogicum in Classical Hebrew*, by J. Hoftijzer. *Journal of Biblical Literature* 106 (1987), 527-528.

11. Review of *Biblical Interpretation in Ancient Israel*, by Michael Fishbane. *Journal of the American Oriental Society* 109 (1989), 679-680.

# AFTERWORDS

## ISAAC RABINOWITZ: A REMINISCENCE
### David I. Owen

It was during my 1988-89 sabbatical, that the sad news of Isaac Rabinowitz's sudden death reached me quickly in Israel via the electronic mail network. In this computer age news, good and bad, travels fast. But Isaac was not of the computer age. He represented the era of pre-World War II scholarship, of meticulous learning, of the mastery of languages and sources, of those who studied at the feet of now legendary masters. Isaac, like his beloved colleague, friend and companion, the late Professor Harry Caplan, was of a kind that will never pass this way again and the Cornell community was fortunate to have had him in its midst for so long. When I joined the Cornell faculty in 1974, Isaac was the first friend I made in the Department of Semitic Languages and Literatures (later renamed Near Eastern Studies) which he had re-established in 1965 after a hiatus of thirty-four years. It was in this department that he trained a handful of students in Hebrew and Arabic who went on to make their marks in their respective fields. He was a trusted colleague and counselor who was always approachable and willing to advise. Characteristically, he never shirked from providing an honest and straightforward opinion even when it meant disagreeing with me. This was an invaluable asset, particularly at times when clear advice was hard to come by.

However, it was Isaac's broad and deep learning that most impressed me. We had long discussions on literary and textual matters, on the role of our discipline in the academy and on the problems of maintaining academic excellence while building and expanding our department. One only had to be present during numerous guest lectures on campus after which the ever-present Isaac would question, comment, and often add brilliant insights, to recognize his ability and breadth. His knowledge ranged over the entire span of Judaica from Biblical through modern Hebrew literature and included Qur'an, Arabic, Syriac, Greek and a host of other languages and literatures that he, at one time or another, had mastered and never forgot. It seemed that he had read nearly every book in his field that entered our library. His incredible recall of minute details, linguistic and literary, virtually unimpaired up to his passing, was indeed a remarkable gift. I shall miss Isaac's daily presence in the Department of Near Eastern Studies, his office door always open to welcome colleagues and students alike interested in discussing one of the many areas in which he read. His legacy to Cornell is the department he built and the students and colleagues he taught and influenced. His presence here constituted another one of the building blocks from which Cornell University is formed. His personal collection of Hebrew manuscripts and rare books, created over a lifetime, now resides in Cornell's magnificent Carl A. Kroch Library, a fitting memorial to one whose life was inseparable from the Hebrew books he loved and to whose comprehension he dedicated his life.

# ISAAC RABINOWITZ: A SCHOLAR'S LIFE

## Ross Brann

Isaac Rabinowitz, Professor Emeritus of Biblical and Semitic Studies at Cornell University died on September 11, 1988, after a brief illness. Isaac was born on July 3, 1909, in Brooklyn, New York, and raised in Kansas City, Missouri. He received an A.B. degree in Greek from the University of California (1929) and a Ph.D. from Yale University (1932) for his dissertation on *The Syriac Versions of Tobit*. Like other young scholars of Semitics of that era, Isaac found many economic and social obstacles standing in the way of his wish to earn a living by doing what he so loved: teaching and research. For the time being he sought to support himself through administrative work, program development and counseling in Jewish communal service and education. At night and on the weekends, however, he continued to satisfy his wide ranging intellectual curiosity by devoting himself to scholarly research. Between 1933 and 1945 Isaac served as Counselor to Jewish Students at Yale University (1933-34); Director of Youth Education for the Union of American Hebrew Congregations (1935-38); Hillel Director at the University of Michigan (1938-40), at Brooklyn College (1940-44), and at the University of Pennsylvania (1944-45), respectively. Next, he worked as National Director of B'nai B'rith Boys Work (1945-46) and as Executive Director of the East New York and Brownsville Young Men's and Young Women's Hebrew Associations (1946-55). In 1946, Isaac married his life's companion, Alice Elson, with whom he had worked professionally at Brooklyn College and later for the B'nai B'rith Youth Organization.

Some twenty-one years after he had earned his doctorate Isaac was finally called to take his rightful place in the academy. It is testimony to his inner strength and determination and to his reputation as a scholar of Semitica that in 1953 Isaac became a Visiting Lecturer in Aramaic at the Hebrew Union College-Jewish Institute of Religion. In 1955 Isaac was named the Lamed (Associate) Professor of Jewish Studies at Wayne State University. Two years later in 1957, Rabinowitz was appointed Professor of Biblical and Hebrew Studies at Cornell University, a position he occupied until his official retirement in 1975. At Cornell, Isaac Rabinowitz was instrumental in the establishment of the Department of Semitic Languages and Literatures (1965) and he served as its Chair from 1965-1970. During his tenure in that office as well as in later years Isaac became an outspoken advocate for an expanded program in Semitics. As he endeavored to build upon Cornell's courses of study in Semitic languages and literatures, two inviolate and interrelated principles guided Isaac's evaluation of academic programs and scholarship. He always insisted upon the necessity of sound philological preparation and the centrality of close textual study in the original languages as the basis of the profession.

Turning to Rabinowitz's erudition and scholarship, one is immediately struck by the seemingly boundless parameters of his learning evident in the list of his scholarly publications appended to this volume. His knowledge of Hebrew literature alone, from the Bible to Bialik, was encyclopedic. More that forty articles and reviews covering many areas of philological, literary, and historical study only suggest the true breadth of learning he commanded. He was at home in Israelite antiquity and biblical literature, in late antiquity and talmudic literature, including Aramaic dialectology; and Isaac's deep appreciation of classical Arabic and Islam, his thorough classical training, and his knowledge of Coptic, Kurdish and many European languages truly distinguished him from the present generation of specialists as well as from his contemporaries whose interests and areas of competence were more narrowly defined.

Isaac's two major works of scholarship serve as eloquent testimony to his elegant style and to his control of method as well as linguistic detail. His critical edition, annotated translation, and study of *Sēpher Nōpheth Ṣūphīm* [*The Book of the Honeycomb's Flow*] (Cornell University Press, 1983), a compendium of Aristotelian and Ciceronian rhetoric by the fifteenth century Italian Hebrew writer, Judah Messer Leon, is an exquisite work of meticulous textual scholarship. Isaac dedicated this book, the product of over twenty years of labor, to his dear friend, the Cornell classicist Harry Caplan, who had encouraged him to undertake and complete the massive project. Isaac's final monograph, *A Witness Forever: Ancient Israel's Perception of Literature and the Resultant Hebrew Bible*, which he dedicated to the memory of his beloved wife Alice, sets forth a highly original explanation of the structure of thought underlying the production of literary texts in ancient Israel. The theory and method developed in this book, it should be noted, were already signaled in Isaac's contribution to L. Wallach, ed., *The Classical Tradition: Literary and Historical Studies in Honor of Harry Caplan* (Ithaca, N.Y., 1966). Now that *A Witness Forever* is finally although posthumously published, Isaac's provocative and highly original semiological approach to the Hebrew Bible will challenge conventional thinking about the way in which language was employed and understood in Israelite antiquity. For work on these two major research projects, Isaac was honored as a Guggenheim Fellow (1961-62) and as a Senior Fellow of the National Endowment for the Humanities (1971-72), respectively.

At Cornell, Isaac was universally admired as a consummate scholar and master teacher. Many younger faculty regarded him as a mentor and friend whose generosity of spirit knew no bounds. Isaac was devoted to the life of the academy in a manner to which many aspired but few, if any, ever achieve. He did not measure success in terms of the number of papers written or in the number of books published, though the quality and range of his written works are extraordinary by any standard. Despite all his professional accomplishments Isaac's inquisitive mind was driven by an intellectual quest in which knowledge itself and interpersonal fellowship were valued more than professional stature. Isaac Rabinowitz was thus dedicated to the life of the mind in its most profound and enduring sense. Academic life signified for him a lifelong process of shared discovery and wonderment—a process in which he was engaged together with his students, his colleagues, and his readers. This meant that he was never too busy or preoccupied to listen and to advise, to read and to critique. And thus when one approached Isaac for guidance and insight, one found him to relish the role of teacher. He was genuinely interested in one's questions and ideas, exacting in his expectations to be sure, but exceedingly gentle in his manner of imparting knowledge and communicating criticism. Isaac was also, in a manner of speaking, the perpetual student absorbed with learning something new. Or perhaps it would be more correct to liken him to the proverbial medieval Seeker since no avenue of critical inquiry, no discipline or historical period was beyond the purview of his intellectual curiosity, manifold interests, and imaginative gifts. How else could an accomplished scholar of Semitic philology, the Hebrew Bible, Aramaic epigraphy and the Dead Sea Scrolls become a brilliant expositor of Hebrew humanism in the Italian Renaissance?

It is a most fitting honor to the memory of Isaac Rabinowitz that his monograph *A Witness Forever* is the inaugural volume in the Occasional Publications Series of the Department of Near Eastern Studies and Program of Jewish Studies, Cornell University.